Saving Father James

Patrick Carney

1st edition 2024

ISBN: 979-8-218-51984-1

DEDICATION

For Megan, the love of my life.

For Abigail and Daniel, always follow your dreams,
and know I love you.

1

The Bridge

Father James Adams was sweating as he loosened the clerical collar on his shirt. His right hand shook as he dug into his pocket, fingers fidgeting around his rosary beads and cough drop wrappers before grabbing his prescription bottle of Ativan.

He sighed with deep disappointment at the sight of the empty bottle in his hand. His fingers, numb from the freezing temperatures, trembled. He didn't even realize when he dropped the bottle on the ground as he stared out at nothing in particular.

His head twitched as if to bring him back to reality. It was officially Christmas morning. Only a few hours earlier, he had celebrated Midnight Mass for a standing-room-only congregation at Saint Mary's Church, two miles from where he now stood.

He looked around, trying to figure out how he'd gotten to the highest point of the Naval Academy Bridge. Large, fluffy snowflakes filled the air. The only sound he heard was the constant and consistent flow of the frigid water of the Severn River 75 feet below. He pulled up his shirt cuff and angled his watch toward the streetlights lining the bridge. 3:46 a.m.

Now, just feet from the edge of the bridge, staring at the beautifully illuminated dome of the Maryland State House in the otherwise clear, dark sky, the pain and guilt weighed on him like an albatross. It was a relentless and gnawing presence that had nestled so deeply within him that it felt like a physical ache in his bones. It pulsed through him. It all came flooding back at once like his life was flashing before his eyes. His mind replayed the events that haunted him.

The truck. The knock. The letter.

The passage of time and changing parishes from state to state helped numb the pain a bit, but the pain and guilt moved with him. He buried it all deep inside and lived an outwardly happy and fulfilling life. At night, or when he was alone, it took its toll for the last twenty years.

Now, after what happened at the end of Mass tonight, it was too much to carry. This was the end. A person can only take so much, he decided.

He stepped closer to the light green railing atop a waist-high brick barrier. The rail, rusted and needing a fresh coat of paint, showed its age and the damage from years of exposure to the elements. His own skin didn't look much better. Wearing just a black, short-sleeve button-down shirt, his arms and face were bright red from the cold wind. He looked down at his fate nearly one hundred feet below. As he looked at the ice-cold, dimly lit water, thoughts raced in his mind.

Will it hurt?

Will it be quick?

Will God understand?

He looked at his watch again. 4:01 a.m.

Standing high above the water, Father James already felt like he was drowning, sinking deeper into a sea of his own making. The pain of the past was not just a memory but a presence that lived within him, a constant companion that colored every moment of joy with shades of sorrow. He felt it now more than ever, pressing down on him with a force that was almost physical, suffocating him with its ferocity.

With another half-step, he was close enough to grasp the railing. Looking down, he saw more than frigid water. He saw the end of his guilt and an escape from what was next. Another breath, as deep as he could manage. He reached his right hand back into his pocket. This time, he grabbed his rosary. Tears filled his eyes and fell down his cheeks. His breathing quickened as the gravity of it all sank in. He began to pray quietly in a voice no louder than a whisper.

"Hail Mary, full of grace, the Lord is with thee. Blessed art thou amongst women, and blessed is the fruit of thy womb, Jesus. Holy Mary, Mother of God, pray for us sinners now and at the ...."

He paused, his eyes darting left and right. A faint sound broke the silence of the bridge in the middle of the night.

Still looking down at the rosary his mother gave him when he entered the seminary, he heard a velvety crunching sound over and over before it abruptly stopped. He glanced up and saw someone hunched over and catching their breath under a streetlamp about 200 feet away. Confused, Father James checked his watch again. Not sure what to do, he just watched and waited.

He saw a young lady in black sweatpants and a black unzipped jacket. Her gray hooded sweatshirt underneath was emblazoned with bright gold lettering reading Navy Cross Country. She was tall with blonde hair pulled back in a ponytail under her blue USNA hat. Her hands were placed on her hips as she continued her trek up the slope of the bridge toward him. He could tell she also wasn't expecting to see anyone on the bridge at this hour on Christmas morning. As she approached, Father James tried to act as normal as possible for a man standing alone atop a bridge in the middle of the night. She gave him an uncomfortable, almost forced smile as she passed him.

The sound of her neon pink and green sneakers crunching through the snow faded away. Relieved that he didn't have to endure an awkward encounter with a stranger, he turned back to his rosary and started over.

"Hail Mary, full of…."

The sound of her sneakers moving through the new-fallen snow abruptly stopped. He kept his eyes closed in hopes that she'd ignore him and move on. A few moments passed, but they both remained still.

"Father James?" she asked.

He sighed in disbelief that he'd run into someone who knew him in this place, at this time. His head turned in her direction. Not sure what to do, he nodded.

"Merry Christmas," he said without even a hint of joy or happiness, hoping his pleasantries would be enough to have her keep walking.

She started walking back toward him.

"I was at Mass with you tonight at Saint Mary's," she said, her smiling face shifting into confusion. "What are you doing out here?"

He paused and thought about why he really was out here. He glanced down at the river below before turning back to her. The clever retort he searched for to explain his actions wasn't coming.

"Oh, just enjoying the peace and quiet," he replied. "I couldn't sleep, and I wanted to clear my head."

He began to cough. He turned his head away from the young lady as the coughing fit continued. He spat what came up from his lungs into the water he'd been studying below.

"You don't have a jacket," she said, as if she was only now noticing. "And that cough doesn't sound good."

She looked at her watch, seeing the hour.

"It's four in the morning," she said, confusion making way for concern. "Are you sure you're alright?"

"Me? Of course. What about you? You're out here alone at night," he deflected as she walked toward him.

Her eyes moved quickly as she assessed the situation. His left hand was still on the railing, his fingers firmly grasping the rosary in his right hand. His shoes were firmly up against the brick wall. His uncovered face and forearms were beet red, showing how long he'd been outside.

Realizing what he looked like, he took a step away from her and removed his hand from the railing. He gave her a less-than-believable smile and pretended that all was well. He knew it was unlikely to work.

"Here, put this on," she said as she removed her jacket. "I've been out for a long run," she said, pointing to her cross country sweatshirt. "I couldn't sleep after Mass, and I have no Christmas plans, so I decided to go for a run. I was hurt and couldn't compete as a Plebe this year. So, I have a lot to prove next fall. No days off for me."

"You keep it," he said, refusing the jacket and hoping to end the conversation. "I'm heading home soon. Good luck next season."

A wave of disappointment fell over Father James when he realized that she wasn't leaving.

"You were crying," she said, squinting to focus on his face and pointing to the remnants of his tears.

Her eyes darted back to his hand on the railing, quickly shifted to the rosary in his hands, and ended up back on his face. They looked at each other in silence. Everything came into focus for her.

"I'm alone on Christmas," she said, attempting to find common ground. "The holidays can be tough when you're alone."

She took another step closer to him when he glanced away to stare blankly at the river below.

"Father James," she said with urgency to break through his disorientation. "Father," she repeated, trying to bring his attention back to her and away from the water. "We don't have to talk, but I'm putting this coat on you."

He didn't reply or even blink. Then, with the coat secure around his shoulders, she stepped between him and the railing.

"Elizabeth," she said in a calm voice, using her left hand to take his. Her right hand touched his face, breaking his focus. "My name is Elizabeth."

He looked down at her and noticed the coat around him. His fading attention turned to frustration.

"You need to go," he said impatiently. "Now."

He stepped quickly toward the railing. He didn't want this young lady to witness his final moments, but it was time. It was time for the pain to end, the guilt to disappear, and to get ahead of the horrors he knew were still ahead.

"I'll go, but I want you to look at this first," she said, removing something from around her neck.

She held out her hand and showed him the crucifix necklace in her palm. Instinctively, he reached out his hand. She forcefully grabbed his forearm, yanked him toward her, and used all her strength to wrap her arms tightly around him, knowing this was the only move she had. She didn't let go.

"I've been through this before," her voice muffled with her face buried in his chest. "You are not alone."

He didn't move or say anything. She just kept hugging him, thinking about her next move. Minutes seemed to pass. The silence was calming but also frightening. It was up to her. Nobody else was coming.

"Please," she said, as she squeezed him even tighter. "Let's go."

As Elizabeth's words hung in the cold air, silence enveloped them. Father James stood motionless, his heart pounding. His eyes glanced down at the water again. He looked down at Elizabeth, a stranger who was holding him tightly. Despite his pain, he was filled with a sense of gratitude that someone had seen his pain and hadn't turned away.

Elizabeth, still holding him tightly, had long wished she wasn't too late the last time. She was determined not to lose this battle.

After a few more seconds, she pushed him away from the railing and pointed his body in the direction of downtown Annapolis, where they both lived. Knowing he had no other choice, he nodded and slowly moved away from the railing.

Elizabeth put her right arm around his back as they took their first steps down the sidewalk along the side of the bridge. Without a word, they walked side by side through the snowy, quiet streets of Annapolis. With each step, the crisp, cold air seemed to bite at their faces, yet the presence of the other provided a silent warmth that countered the harsh December chill. Father James, still numb from the cold and the weight of his thoughts, found unexpected comfort in Elizabeth's presence. For almost forty minutes, they walked in silence. She didn't push him to talk or question him further; she simply walked with him, providing silent support and holding back her unasked questions and unvoiced fears.

As they ascended Newman Street, the incline of the hill forced them to slow their pace. Father James felt each step more acutely, his legs heavy with fatigue. They approached the house where he was temporarily living as the rectory underwent renovations. Elizabeth held the glass storm door open as Father James unlocked the front door.

"Thank you for the jacket," he finally said, deflecting from the true way she helped. He handed the jacket back to her and opened the door.

Elizabeth gave him a small, understanding smile.

"Get some sleep," she said with a motherly warmth.

He nodded and watched as she turned to leave. Before she disappeared into the darkness, he called out, "Elizabeth."

She turned back to him.

"I'm glad you were on the bridge tonight."

Elizabeth's eyes softened, and she simply smiled at him before jogging back down the hill toward the campus of the United States Naval Academy.

Father James ambled up the staircase to his bedroom. He closed the door quietly to avoid anyone hearing him. He walked toward his bed, the rosary still in his hand, and fell to his knees weeping.

Through his tears and prayers, the weight of years of pain and guilt, all of which felt completely deserved, bore down on him. In the dim light of his bedroom, the shadows seemed to press closer, thickening around him like a shroud. His heart throbbed painfully in his chest, each beat a loud drum against the quiet backdrop of the night. The weight of unshed tears from years of suppressed grief and unresolved guilt began to surface, overwhelming him with a torrential force that threatened to sweep him away.

His thumb moved bead after bead of his rosary through his cold fingers. With each bead came a prayer, a plea for forgiveness, and a cry for help.

His thoughts, as they often did during prayer, went back to the truck, the knock, and the guilt he carried. But, it was the pain from just hours earlier that affected him the most on this night. His mind again raced with questions.

Will anyone believe me?

Will my life of faith and good works be tarnished?

What will be my legacy?

Do I have the time and strength to fight?

These are the questions that sent him spiraling toward the bridge. Now, he found enough solace in the kindness, grace, and humanity of a stranger to keep going. He fell asleep a slightly less broken man.

***

As the sunlight from his window landed on his face, Father James slowly opened his eyes. The watch, still on his left wrist from the night before, told him it was almost one o'clock in the afternoon. He sat up abruptly and looked around. He hadn't slept this late without his sleeping pills since he was in college.

He quickly got dressed to head downstairs, wondering what his roommate, the Pastor of Saint Mary's, would think.

"Jim, is that you?" called Father Vincent from downstairs. "You have a visitor."

Confused about the unexpected visitor waiting for him, he adjusted his salt-and-pepper hair, blinked purposefully a few times, and rubbed his hands over his face to tell his body it was time to wake up and act as if nothing happened. He'd hidden his demons for decades. As Father James descended the creaking staircase, his heart thudded uncomfortably against his ribcage, each step amplifying his trepidation. Yet he had conditioned himself to put on a happy face, especially with a visitor waiting for him. Without realizing it, the muscles in his face formed a false smile as he turned the corner at the bottom of the staircase, ready to greet whoever awaited him.

He saw Elizabeth standing up from the living room couch as she placed her mug on the rectangular, mahogany coffee table next to her. She was in her full dress uniform from the Naval Academy, her Plebe Dress Cap with its Navy insignia placed neatly on the table. Well-trained, she stood almost at attention as if an officer was doing a room inspection.

"Elizabeth?" he questioned as the smile left his face.

His heart began to race as the memories of earlier in the morning rushed back.

Why is she here? Did she tell Vincent?

"Good morning, Father," she warmly greeted him. "I made breakfast. Nothing too special. We have French toast, fruit, and a fresh pot of coffee."

"It's the best breakfast we've had in a while," Father Vincent added, confidently sipping his second cup of coffee.

Father James didn't reply or even move from where he first saw Elizabeth. Still stunned at her presence, he was unsure how to act.

"Sit down, I'll fix you a plate," she insisted like an old family friend.

"It's nice to see one of the Midshipmen from your weekly prayer group at the Academy stop by," Father Vincent said. "And, to make us this wonderful Christmas breakfast is such a treat."

He looked up as Elizabeth handed him a full plate with a knowing smile. Relief. She hadn't said anything to Vincent.

"So kind of you, Elizabeth," he said, keeping up his end of the lie. "Thank you."

"A patient young lady, too," Father Vincent added. "She was sitting outside in the cold when I got back from the eleven o'clock Mass. She said she'd been here for a few hours already."

"It was nothing," she interjected, hoping to move the conversation away from the real reason she showed up unannounced.

"I'm going to rest in my room if you don't mind," Father Vincent announced to his colleague and guest. "I'm spent after three Masses this morning. At least I had you to handle midnight. Nice meeting you, Elizabeth, and thank you for this delicious treat."

"Merry Christmas, Father Vincent," she replied.

With bright white hair, a matching short beard, and deep blue eyes covered by his black-rimmed glasses, Father Vincent had been at Saint Mary's for more than a quarter-century. After a recent slip on an icy sidewalk, he moved slowly toward the staircase with his cane and carefully made it up the stairs.

On the living room couch, Father James and Elizabeth sat in silence until they heard the bedroom door close upstairs.

Their eyes met, and Elizabeth could sense the weight of the previous night still on him. She wondered if he would open up about his struggles.

"Thank you very much for breakfast," Father James said, finally breaking the awkward silence. "It's a kind gesture, especially on Christmas."

"You're welcome, Father. I thought you might appreciate a good meal and some company," Elizabeth replied, her eyes warm and comforting.

Father James nodded, and for a moment, they sat quietly, sipping their coffee. He quietly sighed to himself when he realized the decaf coffee would do nothing to help his exhaustion. The room was filled with the warmth of the early afternoon sun and the festive Christmas decorations a few parishioners set up for the priests. Garland lined the mantle on the fireplace where two red stockings with white lettering hung. There was a decorative bowl on the coffee table filled with ornaments and an old, ornate nativity scene on a table adjacent to the front door. The scene was completed by the smell of Christmas cookies, if only from a nearby candle.

While the house seemed to be filled with Christmas cheer, a heaviness lingered inside Father James.

"Elizabeth," Father James began tentatively, "you didn't have to come here. I appreciate the gesture, but I'm not sure I understand why."

She sighed, carefully contemplating her words.

"Father, I saw something last night. I saw a man standing on a bridge, battling something within himself. I saw a broken man who wasn't asking for help but who desperately needed it."

Father James looked down at the breakfast on his plate, which he hadn't touched, a mix of emotions crossing his face. He knew what she'd seen, and it made him uneasy. He had enough guilt already, but now he was also embarrassed.

"Is there something you want to talk about, Father?" Elizabeth asked gently. "Of course, you don't have to confide in me. You don't know me. But, if you want to talk, I'm here."

He hesitated, his eyes meeting hers. At that moment, he saw genuine empathy in her gaze. The defensive walls he'd put up over the years began to show the slightest crack in their foundation.

"I've been carrying a burden for much of my life," he admitted, his voice cracking. "I've lived with this guilt for decades. But the past few days have brought more pain than I can handle. I didn't want the time I had left to be miserable. I didn't want people to remember me for the wrong things."

Elizabeth reached across the table, placing her hand on his.

"You don't have to face it alone," she insisted. "There are people who care about you—people that can help you with whatever you're facing."

Tears welled up in his blue-green eyes as he felt a mix of vulnerability and relief. For years, he had buried his pain deep within, convincing himself that he could and should carry his burden alone.

"Thank you," he said, his voice breaking. "I'm not ready right now, but maybe I can get there."

They sat in silence for a while, the weight of unspoken words lingering in the air. Elizabeth's presence was a lifeline he clung to. As she prepared to leave, Father James walked her to the door. Their eyes met, and he mustered a genuine smile.

Shifting from being comforted to his more familiar role as comforter, Father James looked deeply into Elizabeth's eyes, showing concern.

"It's Christmas," he started, "why aren't you at home with your family?"

Elizabeth hesitated, the question catching her slightly off guard. She shifted slightly, her gaze flickering away for a moment before meeting Father James's concerned eyes again.

"I needed some space this year," she said softly, her voice tinged with an unmistakable undertone of sadness. "The holidays can be tough, you know?"

Her forced smile served as a barrier against the emotions and memories she wasn't ready to discuss. Father James nodded, understanding all too well how the festive cheer could sometimes amplify the shadows in one's heart.

"I do," he replied gently, his voice low and empathetic. "The door is always open here, Elizabeth, no matter the reason."

Elizabeth appreciated the sentiment and offer.

"I should get going," she finally said, breaking the quiet that had settled between them. "A few of us are getting together for a small Christmas dinner tonight."

Father James smiled, his eyes conveying his appreciation for her actions and the time they shared.

"Of course," he said, standing and moving toward the door. "I hope I'll see you again," he said, the words carrying a level of truth he hadn't felt in years.

"I'll be at our weekly prayer group where I always see you," she said with a wry smile, keeping up the ruse she started with Father Vincent.

He watched from the door as Elizabeth began walking back to the Academy. He closed the door and walked back to the living room, where he noticed a wrapped present under the tree that he hadn't seen before.

"For Father James," the tag read. "For when you need a hug. Merry Christmas! Elizabeth."

He opened the box and found the jacket she put over him in his darkest hour. He put the jacket up against his face, a tangible reminder of the unexpected act of love from a stranger, as tears of gratitude formed. He was used to giving comfort, being the rock others clung to in their own storms. But in this quiet moment, with the jacket held tightly up to his face, Father James allowed himself to feel the full extent of his vulnerability and the profound relief of having been seen and saved in his moment of desperation. His life had been full of turmoil for many years, but Father James knew that this life-saving encounter with Elizabeth had to be a turning point for the rest of his life, however short that may be.

2

The Chapel

Eight days after he stood on top of the bridge, Father James emptied his pockets in front of the armed guard he had seen almost every week over the last few years on his visits to the Naval Academy.

"Good evening, Father," called out the tall, muscular guard, Sergeant Ellis, with a smile that reached his eyes.

"How are you doing, Sergeant?" Father James asked as he placed his belongings in the tray. "How was Christmas? Did the kids get everything they wanted?"

"Of course," Ellis replied with a chuckle and a knowing smile. "Santa spoiled them like he does every year."

Father James laughed as he walked through the metal detector and retrieved his pockets' contents.

"How's the knee holding up?" Father James asked.

"Better, thanks for your prayers," Ellis replied. "My wife told me that my men's league basketball days are over."

Father James collected his things from the tray and made his way toward the door to continue on his way.

"Keep praying for me, Father," Ellis said as Father James opened the door, which let in a chill.

"I always do," Father James said with a smile as he stepped outside.

He slowly walked up tree-lined Cooper Road toward his destination. The picturesque snow of the previous week had almost completely melted, leaving behind damp and muddy sidewalks in its stead. On his right, he passed the "Bill the Goat" statue featuring the Academy's beloved mascot and the display of flags honoring each Navy varsity team that defeated Army in their most recent matchup. To the great disappointment of all Midshipmen, a football flag was not among those waving in the breeze after last month's six-point loss to the Cadets.

Walking through the academy's campus known as The Yard, something he'd done each week for years, felt different this time. He noticed his pace had slowed for a few months, but today, he was more winded than usual. Despite the cold temperatures, he found a bench to sit on and catch his breath inside the white, columned Zimmerman Bandstand just across from the chapel.

While he was only 54 years old, his energy had quickly fallen over the last few months. Already tall and skinny, he had lost weight, and his face was gaunt beneath his mostly gray beard. His black rectangular glasses sat over his steel blue eyes just below a faded scar on his forehead. Though his strength and stamina had faded, his mind was still sharp.

He watched the Midshipmen traverse The Yard in a way he hadn't since his early days in Annapolis. The events of the previous week had altered his perspective. Just more than a week ago, he had stood on the brink of oblivion, saved only by the unexpected intervention of a stranger. The memory of that desperate moment, teetering on the edge of the bridge, was still vivid. It had been a turning point, a stark reminder of his mortality and the fleeting nature of time. Despite the pain that brought him to the bridge that night, each day now felt like a gift, a chance to see the world anew.

He watched the Midshipmen hurry from one building to another, their brisk, purposeful strides starkly contrasting with his own faltering steps. The vibrancy of youth, clad in their sharp uniforms that symbolized both honor and immense responsibility, stirred a mix of admiration and sorrow in his heart.

He noticed how young the men and women looked in their pristine uniforms. He thought about what was ahead for each of them, their looming service to their country. War, conflict, and time away from their loved ones. For many, he knew, they were just months away from deployment across the globe. He pictured them on aircraft carriers and destroyers in the Middle East and submarines traveling around the world.

Soon, as had become all too common lately, he felt an overpowering wave of anxiety. A flood of bad memories came back, and he felt on edge as if something terrible was just moments from happening. Seeing the young men and women in their uniforms made him think of his father, Walter, who had served in Vietnam. He knew very little about Walter's experience. From his earlier memories, his father had always been strict and demanding on a good day and angry and abusive on a bad day. He remembered more bad days than good days. Whether it was a result of post-traumatic stress disorder from the war or if his father was just a cruel man, he often wondered, but would never know. Today, he remembered his eighteenth birthday.

***

James and his friend Steve toasted a Miller High Life outside the massive Ben Hill Griffin Stadium, celebrating the 19-6 drubbing of rival Louisiana State. Ranked seventeenth in the country coming into the game, the Gators were led by star running back Emmitt Smith, who rushed for more than 100 yards for the eighth straight game, and a ferocious defense that limited Tigers quarterback Tommy Hodson to 72 yards while forcing three interceptions.

"When Fain took that pick back for a touchdown, it was over!" James said, holding his glass bottle up triumphantly.

"There was no way they were going to come back with Emmitt running the ball like that," Steve added.

The two high school seniors, both hoping to attend the University of Florida next fall, began the long walk home. With a Gators win and a cold beer in hand, the walk didn't bother them at all. As they approached 34th Street, they clinked their drinks one last time as they went their separate ways home.

"Happy birthday, buddy!" Steve shouted from across the street a minute later.

James looked back with a big smile and waved.

A few minutes later, as James walked up to the front door of his ranch-style house, he could hear the familiar sound of his dad screaming at his mom. Looking through the living room window to get a sense of what he was walking into, he saw his mom's face bleeding and bruised. He'd had enough. Today was his eighteenth birthday, and he was a man. He walked past the front door and entered the garage instead. He walked to the large safe in the back of the garage and turned the dial to enter the passcode his father wasn't aware that he knew. He grabbed his dad's shotgun, opened it, and added two shells from the nearby box of ammunition.

Sweating not only from the long day in the sun but also the nerves of walking up to his dad armed, he made his way slowly to the door that led into the house. He stepped inside, the screaming and crying echoing through the home, and carefully walked down the hallway toward his parents.

When he turned into the living room, he saw his mom's beat-up face, but his dad had his back to him and didn't hear him approach. His mom's eyes looked like they would bulge out of her head, and the only sound his dad heard was the sharp metallic click followed immediately by the heavy, clear clack of James cocking the shotgun. His father froze for a few seconds before very carefully turning around.

"Get your hands off my mom," he said in the most defiant moment of his life. "Walk away and get out of this house."

James's hands shook as he tightly gripped the shotgun, the weight of the weapon almost as heavy as the burden in his heart. He felt a surge of anger and fear, his mind racing with memories of every bruise on his mother's face, every trip to the hospital, and every night spent cowering in his room.

"Jimmy, what the hell are you doing?" Walter asked, casually taking a drag from his cigarette as if to dismiss the possibility of his son harming him.

James didn't say a word, but he raised the gun directly at his father.

"Give that to me," his father said sternly, starting to walk across the room toward his son with his hands out. "You know you're not going to shoot me, kid."

"Stay back!" James shouted, conviction replacing fear in his voice. "I'm not a little kid anymore, and you've hurt her for the last time."

"You don't know what you're doing," Walter replied. "You don't have the guts."

The shotgun blast erupted with a thunderous roar, reverberating off the walls and filling the house with a deafening explosion. The acrid smell of gunpowder mingled with the scent of sweat and fear. The deafening silence after the shotgun blast was broken only by the sound of his father's heavy breathing and James's own rapid heartbeat echoing in his ears. Walter stopped immediately with a look of disbelief that his son had just fired a warning shot directly into his favorite recliner that was only a few feet away from him. He looked back at James, stunned, just shaking his head.

"Fine," he finally said, his voice shaking. "You want me to leave. Fine. Goodbye."

James kept the shotgun trained on his father as he backed out of the room, never taking his eyes off the man who had caused so much pain. Walter walked out the front door, slamming it behind him with a finality that echoed through the silent house.

James lowered the shotgun, his arms trembling from the adrenaline, and his legs gave way as he collapsed to the ground. He took a deep breath, feeling the weight of what he had just done settle heavily on his shoulders. He put the gun on the ground and turned to his mom, who was still standing in the corner, her face shocked.

He moved to sit by his mother's side, his hands trembling.

"Mom, are you okay?" he asked, his voice barely above a whisper.

She nodded weakly, tears streaming down her battered cheeks. After decades of making excuses for her husband, she was finally done.

"I'm okay, Jimmy," she said through her tears. "You saved me. I should have left years ago, but I wasn't strong enough. I wanted you to have a father, and …."

"I'm not going to let him hurt you anymore," James said, interrupting his mother, who had nothing to be sorry for. "I'm here for you, and I'm not going anywhere."

His mom, tears streaming down her face, leaned over and embraced him.

"He's still your father, James," she whispered into his shirt, her head pressed up against her son."

"He stopped being my father the day he laid a hand on you," James replied, his voice firm. "I'm a man now, and I'm going to protect you. No one is ever going to hurt you again. Not while I'm here."

They sat there for a moment, holding onto each other. He knew the road ahead would be difficult, but he was ready to face it. For his mom. For himself.

"We'll get through this, Mom," he said. "Together."

As they sat together quietly, the tension of the evening slowly dissipated. The house, a battleground minutes earlier, felt strangely peaceful.

As the adrenaline began to fade, James felt the weight of the day settling on his shoulders. He had crossed a line he could never uncross, but he knew it was the right thing to do. His mom's safety was worth any price.

Later that night, after his mom went to bed, he returned to the living room and stared at the shotgun. Still shocked that he actually fired the weapon, he looked at it and felt that he took the power his father held over his family from him. He removed the remaining ammunition and locked it back in the safe.

As the days passed after James's birthday, he and his mom expected that Walter was just holed up with a friend, trying to let the situation blow over for a few days. As those days came and went, turning into weeks, James found himself replaying the scene over and over in his mind. The sound of the shotgun blast haunted his dreams, and he couldn't shake the fear that his father might return. But he also felt a newfound strength, a resolve to protect his mother at all costs.

News of the confrontation spread quickly through their Towne Parc neighborhood. While some neighbors offered support and encouragement, others cast judgmental glances, their whispers cutting like knives. James walked through it all with his head held high, determined to rise above the gossip and protect his mother.

After a while, James and his mom moved on, and Walter never returned. As the days turned to weeks, months, and eventually years, James and his mom almost never spoke of him again. It was as if they took an eraser to all memories of him.

***

Thirty-six years later, Father James sat on a Naval Academy bench with a very different perspective on life. He hoped there was a time when his father loved him and his mother, but none came to mind. As sad as it would be, part of him wished his father's behavior was a casualty of war. At least he could rationalize that soldiers coming home from Vietnam didn't have the same access to mental health resources that are commonplace now. These young men and women were dedicated to serving their country, just as his father had been. Modern war was still hell on Earth, but unlike in his father's time, today's soldiers had an improved support system and returned to a community that seemed to understand the importance of mental health. Some of these young men and women would give their lives or limbs for their country, but nobody would come back the same as they left. He thought about the contrast between the homecoming his father and other Vietnam veterans received compared to the experiences of modern soldiers. Many Vietnam veterans were scorned when they came home and were treated like pariahs without the support or understanding they needed to heal. In contrast, today's soldiers, sailors, and Marines

[29]

rightfully came home to a hero's welcome from a grateful country that valued their well-being.

Father James wondered how different his life might have been if his father had received the help he needed after he returned from Vietnam. Would there have been less anger and fewer nights filled with fear and violence? The scars of war were evident in his father's eyes, a haunting emptiness that James had only begun to understand as he grew older. He also considered the possibility that his dad was just not a good man. Every time he thought back to his childhood, it was the unknown that always gnawed at him.

Trying to quell the anxiety, Father James focused on his breathing and tried to bring himself back to the present moment as the Midshipmen traversed The Yard. After a few minutes, he forced himself to forget the past, stand up, and move forward. As he stood up from the bench, he was glad that he could play a small role in supporting even a few of the Midshipmen. Steadying himself with a deep breath, he resumed his walk. The crisp air tugged at the edges of his thin jacket, not quite warding off the chill that seeped into his bones. He pulled the fabric closer around himself as a shield from the biting wind that swept across the open spaces of The Yard. He noted the historic buildings of the Academy with their imposing structures and stoic facades, standing as silent sentinels over the young lives that passed through their halls. Each corner of The Yard held years of memories from Midshipmen who had walked these same paths for generations.

He finished his walk and found himself in the friendly and familiar confines of the Brigade Chapel. After taking a moment to catch his breath and genuflect at the altar, Father James slowly climbed the curved staircase to the balcony where his group would meet. In the minutes he had before his solitude ended, Father James sat in the sacred silence of the chapel, surrounded by a profound sense of solitude that both comforted and confronted him. As he waited for the arrival of his prayer group, Father James's thoughts drifted involuntarily back to the bridge and to Elizabeth, the unexpected guardian who had pulled him back from the brink. The contrast between the despair he had felt that night and the tranquility of the chapel was jarring. Here, surrounded by symbols of faith and peace, he struggled to reconcile the darkness of that night with the meticulously decorated chapel. The US Navy flags that hung from the balcony underscored the chapel's role not merely as a house of worship but as a custodian of naval honor and history.

Behind and below him, the rest of the magnificent 2,500-seat chapel sat empty and peacefully quiet. The chapel and its iconic dome had served as a landmark for Midshipmen and Annapolitans for more than 115 years. Its rich blue carpet ran down the nave of the church, surrounded by old but well-cared-for mahogany wood pews topped with cushions to match the carpet. The chapel would still be decorated with ornate and festive Christmas decorations for a few more days. Three lit Christmas trees and at least a dozen poinsettias decorated the altar, while the manger with Mary, Joseph, and baby Jesus sat illuminated by a light. The organ, with five rows of keys and countless knobs on either side that brought God's word to life, sat peacefully silent. The ornate pulpit, which required the preacher or lector to ascend three steps to the top, was adorned with a magnificent wreath and a red ribbon. The chapel was a remarkable building, but it never looked better than at Christmastime.

He stood as he heard the first of the nearly two dozen Midshipmen begin to arrive from dinner. They had come after a long day that started with the sound of a trumpet playing the morning Reveille at 6:30 a.m. Now, they quietly sat down to listen to and discuss scripture as a group. Some of the Midshipmen came from very religious families and knew the Bible chapter and verse. Others were seeking to cultivate a relationship with God, knowing the dangers ahead. To Father James, all were welcome.

Behind the Midshipmen, overlooking the group, was the Sampson Window. Mainly featuring light blue and yellow, the Winged Angel of Peace stood as the centerpiece of the spectacular stained-glass window. Above the Angel, seven individual windows spread out like a peacock's feathers. Father James had picked this spot years ago when he began his weekly meetings not just for the beauty of the chapel below but as a prayer for peace for those willing to go to war. The colors of the window, illuminated by the soft glow of the setting sun, bathed the chapel in a serene light, providing a sense of calm and reflection that Father James hoped would resonate with the young men and women under his spiritual guidance. As the Midshipmen settled into the pews, Father James felt a sense of normalcy after a chaotic week.

Because of the holiday, it had been two weeks since his prayer group had gathered. Much of his time, especially when alone, was filled with guilt, tormenting memories, and fear for his future, he genuinely enjoyed his time each week with the Midshipmen. Since he first started working on his ordination after college, he'd always been drawn to working with young people. He appreciated and now envied their energy, hopefulness, and less jaded worldview. He saw value in reaching people when they were young and had the rest of their lives ahead. Still, working with Midshipmen was unique because of their combination of gifted intellect and commitment to serving others.

Father James used the new year as a device to reflect on the past and the present. His message, he hoped, would help the young men and women gathered there. In reality, he was his own audience. After his fateful trip to the bridge, he'd spent a lot of time reflecting on this theme. In his years as a priest, he'd often given people advice about moving on from tragedy and embracing present opportunities. He just never followed his own guidance. He was ready, he thought, to begin the unburdening process.

"As we step into a new year, it's common to reflect on the year behind us and plan for what lies ahead," Father James began, his gaze sweeping across the youthful faces before him. "I invite each of you to share, not just your triumphs, but also your trials. Today, I want us to speak about the weights we carry—guilt, grief, or even uncertainty about the future. We are stronger together than we are alone."

A young Midshipman, who seemed burdened by more than the weight of a military career, spoke first.

"I lost my mother just a few months ago," he shared, his voice steady but low. "The doctors caught the cancer too late, and she was gone only a few months after the diagnosis. It was so sudden that there weren't any treatment options that would work for her. The grief comes in waves, and sometimes it's paralyzing. But being here with all of you helps me feel less alone. I think the fact that she was gone so quickly made it harder because I couldn't prepare, if that's even possible."

Nods of understanding rippled through the group as a young woman stood up to take her turn.

"I'm just a Plebe," she started. "And, this is harder than I thought it would be. I'm struggling with the decision to continue my service or start something new."

A few more senior Midshipmen chimed in and shared how they overcame their Plebe year difficulties and offered support.

Father James listened intently, offering words of comfort or a thoughtful nod, encouraging them to delve deeper.

'It's brave to voice your doubts and fears," he reassured them. "I'm sure you're not the only person who had those fears as a Plebe."

A number of the older Midshipmen nodded their heads in agreement.

As the hour unfolded, more midshipmen shared their stories. Some spoke of the intense pressure of expectations, others about personal battles with mental health. Between their stories, Father James shared his reflections, drawing from his own reservoir of unresolved challenges.

"I've often told others to embrace the present and let go of the past," he confessed, his voice tinged with a vulnerability that he rarely allowed himself to show. "Yet I struggle with this myself. Like many of you, I'm learning that the first step in overcoming our battles is acknowledging them."

The room grew quiet, a shared silence that was comforting and reflective. It was a moment of collective vulnerability and strength, a rare pause in their rigorous lives. He didn't expand further on his personal issues but felt good for even broaching the topic.

"Thank you all for your honesty today," Father James said, as the session neared its end. "Our shared experiences, the burdens, and the breakthroughs remind us that we're not alone. Whether it's in our relationship with Christ or our brothers and sisters here, we can draw strength from places other than ourselves. We carry not just our own strength but the strength of every voice shared here today."

He thought about how he had never followed his own advice and about how that had to change. He looked down at his Bible, where he'd been wearing down the pages in the Book of Philippians, as he read the same Bible verse all week, thinking about his time on the bridge and his encounter with Elizabeth. If he closed his eyes for more than a second or two, he was back on the bridge, looking straight down at the frigid water below. Father James knew that he would never truly be able to move forward without the closure found in sharing his story, even if this wasn't the proper setting.

"I'm so glad to see so many of you here this evening," Father James said, wrapping up the hour-long gathering. "As we do each week, we'll close with one final reading of the verses we discussed tonight. Let's bow our heads, feel the calming silence, and ground our thoughts as we prepare for the week ahead and make a plan to put the message of these words into action each day."

He excused himself for a minute as a coughing fit ensued, breaking the silence he had just asked for. The fits were becoming too familiar and weighed on him. He took the final sips from a water bottle he carried with him, caught his breath, and placed a cough drop in his mouth before beginning to read the verse that had stayed with him all week.

Brethren, I count not myself to have apprehended: but this one thing I do, forgetting those things which are behind, and reaching forth unto those things which are before. I press toward the mark for the prize of the high calling of God in Christ Jesus.

He paused for a few moments to let the words sink in. The extended silence, he believed, punctuated the significance of the words.

After a quiet moment, he sent the Midshipmen off with a blessing and exchanged pleasantries with the group as they departed. A Midshipman named Emily, a constant presence in the chapel each week, approached and handed him a bag.

"For you and Father Vincent to enjoy," she said with a smile before returning to her seat to collect her things.

Looking into the bag, Father James saw a package of homemade peanut butter blossom cookies wrapped neatly in cellophane with a red bow on top.

"Thank you," he said with a smile of appreciation. "Father Vincent and I will put these to good use with a tall glass of milk."

As Emily left with a smile, Father James sat alone on the balcony overlooking the chapel, listening to the bustle of the Midshipmen heading home. He knew this was the first step. It helped to see others demonstrate the courage to share dark moments in their lives. Whether it was a therapist, Father

Vincent, or a friend, he knew it was time to unshackle himself from decades of mental torment.

He looked back, hearing someone approach. He turned back toward the stained-glass window, but his eyes quickly diverted toward Elizabeth. She stood there with a friendly yet uncertain smile.

"I wasn't sure if I should come here tonight," Elizabeth admitted. "But I wanted to check in on you."

Father James smiled to assure her that he was happy she had come. He'd thought of Elizabeth more than anyone else over the past eight days. She saved his life and showed genuine compassion to a stranger at his lowest moment.

"It's wonderful to see you," he said, smiling. "I've thought of you often since we last spoke."

She smiled, unsure of what to do next.

"Please," he motioned toward her, "sit down with me."

"How are you?" Elizabeth asked after a few moments of taking in the peaceful surroundings.

"I'm not doing well," he answered with a smile that didn't match his words. "But that's the best answer I could have hoped for. I'm here, and I'm willing to tell someone how I really am."

He placed his hand on top of hers, giving it a meaningful squeeze to thank her.

"You know my most intimate secret, and I don't even know your last name or anything about you," he said, chuckling at the oddity of their relationship.

"Elizabeth Fitzgerald," she said, awkwardly extending her hand for a formal handshake. "Nice to meet you."

Their laughter at the uncomfortable exchange broke the tension in the otherwise empty chapel.

"I grew up on a dairy farm in Vermont," she said. "In a small town that nobody's heard of next to the Canadian border."

She told Father James all about the 250 Holsteins her family milked and how her favorite job was caring for the calves. For a while, they chatted about life on the farm and family.

"What brought you here, to the Academy?" he asked.

"I guess I'm running from some things in my past too," she said, her tone changing. "I needed something new, a fresh start."

He gave her a look of compassion as his pastoral instincts kicked in. He was eager to switch to a more familiar role and serve as a counselor to his new friend.

"I never saw myself in the military," she continued. "I started getting noticed by colleges for cross country, and Navy recruited me. I visited, and I fell in love."

He smiled as she paused.

"What about you, Father?" she countered. "Are you from Maryland?"

"Florida, actually," he answered. "I lived down there until I graduated from college and entered the seminary."

He told her about life growing up in Gainesville, a college town in north-central Florida. He went on about how he spent Saturdays with his friend Steve at The Swamp watching the Gators. The rabid fans, full stadium, and vibrant blue and orange colors all over town helped develop a passion for sports.

Father James still remembered the Charley Pell years fondly. Despite being fired the following season for NCAA infractions, he led the team to a memorable win over Iowa in the 1983 Gator Bowl. Steve's dad drove them out to Jacksonville, and their seats were near the end zone where Neal Anderson scored the opening and decisive touchdown against the Hawkeyes.

"So, how did you end up here in Annapolis?" Elizabeth asked.

"After ordination, I became a parish priest in New Jersey," he said, his tone shifting from the excitement of recounting his favorite Gators football memories. "But after a few years, I also needed a change of scenery. Eventually, that brought me here."

He knew telling her it was a change of scenery was an understatement, but he hoped it sufficed for now.

"Something happened to you in New Jersey," she said with a mix of confidence and concern.

Elizabeth's words, truer than she knew, cut through the air with surgical precision, pinpointing a buried segment of his past. He met her gaze, and in her eyes, he saw not just curiosity but the deep, unwavering empathy he had seen just eight days earlier. It was as if she could see straight through to his soul and the tangled mess of regrets and unresolved pain he carried with him. In that moment, Father James experienced a tumult of emotions. The memory of New Jersey brought a rush of images he usually kept locked up behind mental barricades. He saw flashes of faces and places and heard echoes of kind voices and sorrowful wails, all swirling around that pivotal, painful chapter of his life.

There was an instinctual urge to deflect, to retreat behind the well-rehearsed pleasantries that had long served as his armor. But, looking into Elizabeth's earnest and concerned face, something shifted within him. Here was someone who had seen his darkest moment and had literally pulled him back from the edge. Could he really continue to wear his mask in front of her?

Feeling an unfamiliar mixture of vulnerability and relief, he acknowledged her observation with a nod, a simple gesture that felt like he was unloading a small part of the heavy burden he carried. The silence that followed was thick with anticipation, charged with the unspoken understanding that they might be on the precipice of a more profound revelation. He was so comfortable being on this side of the conversation. But, in twenty years, he hadn't talked about his time in New Jersey to many people.

The verse from Philippians echoed through his thoughts, a beacon in the fog of his hesitations: "Forgetting those things which are behind, and reaching forth unto those things which are before." It was a call to move forward, to unburden himself of the past that haunted him.

The chapel's serene atmosphere, underscored by the protective gaze of the Winged Angel of Peace, seemed to offer a safe harbor for his confession. As the weight of his memories pressed down on him, Father James felt a rare stirring of resolve. He thought back to the bridge a week earlier. It was time to share, to unload the heavy cargo of his past that he had carried in solitude for far too long.

Elizabeth knew she had hit a pain point and waited in silence for Father James to be ready to share. She didn't want to push him into something he wasn't prepared for, but she wanted to be ready to listen. They sat in silence for a while as he sought the courage to begin.

It was time to share. It was time to confess.

"October 12, 2003," he said, abruptly breaking the quiet.

3

The Dance

His palms are sweaty, knees weak, arms are heavy. There's vomit on his sweater already, Mom's spaghetti.

The music in the cafeteria blasted as nearly fifty teenagers shouted the lyrics to Eminem's anthem "Lose Yourself." At least the girls promised it was the radio edit of the song, Father James thought. The last thing he needed was Father Brendan, his parish's pastor, making an unannounced visit to the charity dance marathon and hearing the teens of his parish's youth group screaming the F-bombs in Eminem's new song.

Father James actually enjoyed the song and played it on a CD with headphones on at the rectory. It was upbeat and catchy. Despite some language he wouldn't have chosen, it had a great message about seizing the moment.

At 34 years old, Father James had only been an ordained priest for two years. Unlike most priests, he was young and more relatable to the youth in the community. He liked sports, modern music, and was always full of energy. He often joined the teens for basketball games, quoted popular songs in his homilies, and could always be found with a smile on his face. The teens in the church's youth group appreciated his unique perspective and knew they could come to him for advice about anything. Whether it was school stress, relationship troubles, or even questions about faith, Father James had a way of making them feel heard and understood. His approachability and genuine interest in their lives created a bond that made each of them feel special.

Most of his friends were either engaged or married, and his college roommate had a newborn girl and a two-year-old boy. His friends were teachers, accountants, and engineers. One friend was an Air Force pilot, and another had just opened his own orthodontic practice.

As Father James observed his friends' lives unfolding along traditional paths—marriages blossoming, children's laughter filling their homes—he couldn't help but reflect on the path he had chosen. The life of a priest demanded sacrifices that were at once profound and invisible to those outside the clergy. He had willingly foregone the personal milestones of marriage and fatherhood, along with the intimate joys and challenges they brought. Each gathering with friends was a stark reminder of the life he might have had, full of familial love and the chaos of raising children.

Yet, when he spent time with his friends, Father James found a unique comfort in his vocation. His life was filled with purpose and spiritual fulfillment. He found joy in guiding the youth of his parish, offering them counsel and spiritual direction. His energy and modern touch didn't just make him a figure of authority; they made him a confidant and mentor. The connection he felt with his parishioners, especially the younger ones, provided him with a sense of family that, while different from his friends' experiences, was deeply rewarding. He often thought about the many rewarding moments he shared with his youth group—their accomplishments, their struggles, their growth—and felt a profound sense of gratitude. His calling would give him a unique kind of legacy, one built not on blood relations, but on the hearts and minds he helped shape. Some of his friends didn't understand, but he was happy and fulfilled.

While the teens were able to relate better to a young priest, the rest of the congregation certainly noticed his age when he first arrived. When he was first introduced at the church, a few older parishioners asked where the real priest was or thought the baby-faced priest was an old altar server. His quick wit and insistence on not taking himself too seriously allowed him to embrace their questions and answer them with self-deprecating jokes.

He looked around the room and smiled, watching the teens sing and dance, and it brought back memories of his time in high school. He could almost feel the humid air on his skin as he remembered those balmy Florida nights, the kind where the heat lingered long after the sun had set.

Though not quite a mullet, his hair was long and thick in the back, a great contrast to his current conservative hairstyle. He could see himself arriving at a high school dance wearing a faded pair of jeans with a sports coat at least a size too big, with the sleeves rolled up. He'd be hanging with the guys, talking about what girl they wanted to dance with and singing at the top of their lungs when U2's "Where the Streets Have No Name" or "Born in the U.S.A." by Bruce Springsteen came on the speakers. After every dance, he'd drive his friends in his light blue 1970 Plymouth Duster to Arnold's Pizzeria on University Avenue. It was their haven, a place where they could just be kids. Before the shop closed at midnight, they'd each grab one last slice and a Coke to enjoy in the dimly lit parking lot. They'd talk about everything and nothing—the girls at school, how they'd stay friends forever, and what the future held for each of them. Even then, he understood how special those nights at Arnold's were with his friends.

Father James laughed to himself at the thought of telling his teenage self, sitting on the hood of his Duster, that he'd become a priest just 15 years later.

Suddenly, the sound of the teens singing "Say it Ain't So" from Weezer's 1994 self-titled album across the hall brought him back to the present.

The song brought him back to the week before he took his final vows. His friends from Florida came up to Philadelphia to visit and take him out for a fun night. It was his version of a bachelor party, they told him. They waited outside of the Electric Factory for hours to get as close to the front as possible when Weezer took the stage. He could still close his eyes and see Rivers Cuomo, just feet away, rocking out to "Buddy Holly." Now, just a few years later, he was in the Catholic elementary school cafeteria that doubled as a hangout for his high school youth group, enjoying the same songs as a few dozen high school students who were energetically moving and singing.

Slowly and unexpectedly, Father James walked to the center of the dance floor and began belting out the chorus.

Say it ain't so, your drug is a heartbreaker. Say it ain't so, my love is a life taker.

The chorus ended with an eruption of cheers. There was something extra fun about a priest joining in on the party and giving them a glimpse of James Adams, the person behind the collar. He didn't want to be a boring, reserved priest. He tried to use his youth to form a connection with the teens of the community he served.

The clock on the cafeteria wall read 11:15 p.m. He needed to take a break if he was going to last until the dance marathon ended at 7 a.m.

A group of teens from the youth group had been planning the dance marathon since the beginning of the school year. They volunteered each month in a food pantry in nearby Camden, and they wanted to find a way to raise money to help feed those in need. Friends, family, and neighbors sponsored the teens for the number of hours they danced. There was also a 50/50 raffle the teens had sold tickets for after Masses since late September.

As Father James stepped into the hallway between the cafeteria and gymnasium to catch his breath, he was greeted by cheers and high-fives from the teens. He made his way to the refreshment table, where he found a stack of pizza boxes, bowls filled with chips, and cans of soda. The aroma of cheese and tomato sauce filled the air, making him realize how hungry he was. He grabbed two slices and a Wild Cherry Pepsi before finding a spot on a bench in front of the gym. Just as he took a big bite of pizza, the three girls who organized the event seemed to appear in front of him, overflowing with excitement.

Jess Taylor was the group's leader. Petite with blonde hair and big, stunning blue eyes, she was the kind of girl who could light up a room with her smile. Her charisma was magnetic, drawing people into her orbit with a warm, engaging manner that made each of her classmates feel uniquely seen and important.

Jess always showed up with perfectly curated outfits. Her dream was to work in the fashion industry in Manhattan and eventually design her own clothing line. She devoured fashion magazines with the same intensity that some of her classmates applied to sports statistics or video games.

Her passion, drive, and organizational skills all worked in her favor. As a senior, she would soon be sending out her college applications to Philadelphia University and Drexel University, both known for great fashion programs in nearby Philadelphia, sitting at the top of her list. Manhattan was her dream, but she wasn't ready to be too far from her family. She always reminded Father James that family was her top priority when he inquired about her college search. In her interactions with him, Jess always spoke with a mixture of reverence and excitement about her future plans. She respected his guidance, finding in him a patient listener and a thoughtful adviser. Father James, in turn, was struck by her maturity and her clarity of purpose. It was rare, he thought, to meet someone so young who was so sure of what she wanted and so dedicated to achieving it.

Jess was technically the middle of three children, as her twin brother, who was dancing with his girlfriend across the hall, was born three minutes earlier. Her younger brother, Jason, would start high school next year. Jess's relationship with her family played a crucial role in her decision-making process. She adored her parents and shared a special bond with her younger brother, Jason, whom she was both protective of and immensely proud of. This closeness made the idea of moving far away for school somewhat daunting. Philadelphia University offered her an ideal compromise—a stepping stone toward her ultimate goal, allowing her to stay connected with her family while pursuing her ambitions.

If Jess was around, Lauren Rodriguez and Maggie Mitchell were never far behind. Both juniors, Lauren and Maggie seemed to move in a pack with Jess.

"Father James!" Jess shouted, wearing a proud smile across her face as they approached. "Guess how much money we raised?"

He pointed to his mouth, full of pizza, to avoid being impolite. He wasn't sure if she wanted him to guess. She may not have even listened if he did. She was bursting with excitement and had to get it out.

"Two thousand," Jess paused after really emphasizing 'thousand,' "four hundred and seven dollars!"

He quickly swallowed his pizza and stood up.

"I'm so proud of each of you," he said, standing to give each of them a hug. "That will help so many people who need a meal."

"We gotta go tell everyone," Jess squealed as they ran like a pack back into the cafeteria that sounded like a nightclub.

Moments like this reinforced his decision to enter the priesthood. He was making a real connection with people and helping those in need.

The dance continued as Saturday night turned into Sunday morning. He danced a little more and spent some time across the hallway in the gym, where a few guys started a middle-of-the-night game of pickup basketball.

With the sound of everything from Green Day to Britney Spears as their backdrop, the gym echoed with the sounds of sneakers squeaking on the polished floor and the rhythmic bouncing of the ball. Father James joined in and showed off a decent jump shot for a priest.

As the night progressed, Father James took breaks to chat with the teens and shared stories from his own high school days in the 80s. The camaraderie and pizza got him through the early morning hours.

Seeing the dance floor thinning out and the energy fading with only thirty minutes to go, he had the DJ throw on one of his favorite 1980s power ballads, "Don't Stop Believin'" by Journey. He took the microphone and started to sing.

Just a small town girl, livin' in a lonely world, she took the midnight train going anywhere. Just a city boy, born and raised in South Detroit, he took the midnight train going anywhere.

This got the energy back up, even if just to take a chance to laugh at their group's leader. He handed the microphone back when everyone started singing along.

His plan worked as the teens kept their energy up enough to reach the finish line of the dance marathon at 7 a.m.

"Are you coming out for breakfast, Father?" Jess asked as they cleaned up the empty pizza boxes and soda bottles.

"Oh, I don't think so," he said, with sleep on his mind. "You go with your friends and have fun."

"You have to come," Jess insisted. "We're all going over to Dottie's Diner. The whole group."

He looked at the clock and sighed. He hadn't slept in 24 hours.

"Alright," he said. "I'll come for...."

She didn't let him finish.

"Great!" Jess interjected, giving him a hug. "Can I ride with you? Justin wants to drive his girlfriend without his sister hanging around."

"Of course," he replied. "Let me get my things."

He walked over to the school's office and picked up his keys and dark blue Nokia cell phone. He wrapped himself in his warm, brown leather jacket and met up with Jess in the hallway.

"I am hungry," he said, warming to the idea of going to Dottie's for breakfast. "There's a short stack, home fries, and a cup of coffee in my future."

He locked up the school building and walked with Jess across the parking lot to the rectory. The two-story brick building was home to Father James and Father Brendan as well as to the parish offices and meeting rooms. The rectory showed its age, but it served its purpose. Two priests who'd taken vows of poverty didn't need much.

Their neighbors in the community around them were just waking up to start their Sunday. A few cars even began pulling into the parking lot in preparation for the first Mass of the day. Father James was grateful that Father Brendan agreed to cover each Mass today in support of his sleep-deprived colleague.

He unlocked the doors of his 1996 Mercury Sable. The red exterior was worn, and the dents from a few fender benders still showed. He'd had the car for less than two years, and the damage was already there, but he would often point to the car and remind his youth group teens about his vow of poverty with a laugh.

"Are you alright being seen in this car?" he asked with a smile. The teens often teased him about it.

"To Dottie's," she said, pointing with excitement. "Get this homely holy roller going!"

They both laughed as he started the engine.

He pulled out of the parking lot and began heading toward the diner. There wasn't a cloud in the sky, just the bright, beautiful early morning sun.

Jess began talking about her college search and the schools she was still considering. Her energy was incredible. Along with Lauren and Maggie, she had arrived early for the 12-hour dance marathon to set up. Now, after being awake all night, she was still her usual perky self. The Energizer Bunny, he often thought.

Father James heard what she was saying but admittedly wasn't hanging on every word. He wanted to eat and go back to the rectory for some much-needed sleep.

The car finally began to warm up on the unusually cold October morning as he pulled up to the intersection with Route 73, which would take him right to the diner. The light turned red moments before he got there, and he knew it would be a minute or two before the light turned green.

Father James felt a moment of peace amidst his exhaustion as the warmth from the heater and the morning sun relaxed him. He squinted and then closed his eyes to get a short respite from the blinding morning sun. Jess's ongoing chatter about college plans, usually engaging, now just blended with the low hum of the idling car and the rhythm of the turn signal, creating comforting background noise. His shoulders relaxed as he sank further into the driver's seat, waiting for the light to turn green as Jess kept talking.

"That's why Justin wants to move far away for college," she said, Father James not hearing a word. "If you want to move across the country, fine. Just go!"

Father James's eyelids fluttered open as Jess's voice reached a crescendo, her last two words snapping him back to the present. He blinked rapidly, the harsh sunlight flooding his vision with white, disorienting light. For a split second, he felt the overwhelming brightness dominate his senses, forcing him to squint as he struggled to refocus his eyes on the road and his surroundings.

Instinctively, his hands tightened on the steering wheel as his eyes still worked to adjust to the intrusive sunlight. His right foot, previously relaxed against the brake pedal at the red light, now shifted decisively to the accelerator. As he maneuvered the car left in the diner's direction, his head jerked to the right, hearing Jess's piercing scream. Time seemed to slow as he turned to look at Jess.

Then, he saw the truck.

***

"How are you feeling, James?" called out an unfamiliar voice. "Honey, you're going to be fine."

Fine from what, he tried to figure out, struggling to open his eyes. His head was throbbing worse than any headache he'd ever experienced.

"Keep your hands down," the voice said as he felt his forehead. "I'm almost done with the stitches."

"No," he said, confused. "I need to go to the diner."

The mention of the diner triggered his brain. His mind raced with thoughts bouncing from one to the next. The dance, the car ride, the truck. His eyes opened widely as the heart monitor alarm at his bedside sounded, warning of his rapidly increasing heart rate.

"Jess!" he screamed. "Where's Jess?"

As his eyes finally adjusted to the light, he saw the woman whose voice he'd heard casually fastening a bandage to his forehead, as if she'd done it many times before.

"Who's Jess?" she asked, taking off her blue medical gloves. "Was she in the car with you?"

"Yes," he replied frantically. "Yes, the car. Jess was in the car with me. I need you to tell me where she is."

"Let me check, honey," said the lady, who he would later realize was his doctor in the emergency department, as she stepped away.

He looked down to find his shirt ripped open and covered in blood. He was alone, lying on a hospital bed surrounded by beige privacy curtains. The sounds of the emergency department surrounded him— beeping, groaning, orderlies pushing beds down the hallway. The fluorescent lights beamed too brightly above him.

He closed his eyes to focus his thoughts and replayed the events in his mind. He saw the kids dancing and laughing with Jess about the condition of his car. She was right next to me, he thought. He remembered her scream and the look of terror in her eyes. He remembered the truck. He replayed the accident in his head. The truck was going straight through the intersection and would have hit her side.

"Jess!" he screamed out with anguish, hoping she could hear him from a nearby room. "Jessica!"

"Sir, you need to calm down," said a nurse who came rushing in. "Your heart is racing, and you have a concussion. You need to rest."

"Where's Jess?" he pleaded, staring directly into her eyes.

"Your doctor just went to check," she said, trying to calm him. "It was just you they brought in, honey. Is Jess your daughter?"

"Daughter?" he questioned. "No. I'm her priest. We were leaving the church. She was in the car with me."

The nurse quickly turned away so he wouldn't notice how her face fell when she heard the word 'priest.' She'd heard about the accident with a priest, but he was wearing jeans and a button-down shirt, and she didn't realize who he was.

As his thoughts raced, his heart monitor kept pace. The only one they brought in? Maybe she's okay, he thought. She's young and healthy, so maybe she just got a few bumps and scrapes. He closed his eyes to pray.

"Heavenly Father, watch over Jess and keep her safe."

His prayer quickly turned into a negotiation with God in his mind when he heard a familiar voice in his room.

"Father, are you okay?" said the voice, interrupting his thoughts.

He opened his eyes to see Ann Lombardi, his parish's secretary, hurrying into the room with his doctor.

"Ann," he said with surprise in his voice. "Where's Jess?"

"Oh, Father," she said as she bent over to gently hug him.

"Father Adams," his doctor said stoically until their eyes met. "I'm very sorry to tell you that Jess didn't survive the crash. The paramedics pronounced her at the scene before getting you to the hospital. I'm sorry."

In the moments after the doctor's words cut through the air with finality, Father James felt the room, with its sterile white walls and the incessant beeping of machines, close in around him, each beep echoing the shattering of his world. The air thickened, each breath becoming more difficult than the last.

His vision blurred, and he felt as if he had been abruptly cast into a surreal nightmare. The sounds around him—the buzzing of the medical staff, the soft sobbing of Ann beside him—merged into a distant, unrecognizable drone.

Ann, still holding him gently so as not to cause more pain, began to weep, her tears absorbed by Father James's bloody shirt. Father James stared straight ahead in disbelief. Without blinking, tears began falling down his stunned face. His hearing seemed to sharpen and then fade, the murmurs of the medical staff and Ann's soft sobbing weaving into a cacophony that seemed both distant and piercingly close. The room felt oppressively small as if the very air he breathed was thickening, making each inhale an effort fraught with emotional and physical pain. He felt a cold sweat break out across his forehead as his heart thumped against his chest as if trying to escape the unbearable weight of his sorrow.

Suddenly, his head jerked toward the doctor as a terrified expression filled his face. In his anguish, he lashed out, his body moving violently and unpredictably. Thrashing, he shoved away the hands that reached out to steady and comfort him.

Without warning, he felt the sharp sting of the nurse's needle. As the sedative coursed through his veins, dulling the edges of his agony, his body began to sink slowly back onto the pillow. His mind, fighting against the encroaching darkness, verbalizing his singular, torturous thought.

"Forgive me, God, I killed her."

4

The Guilt

ather James and Elizabeth sat silently in the first row of the Brigade Chapel balcony. The silence was only broken by the sound of her sniffles and her hands wiping tears from her eyes. A man she barely knew had just unburdened himself of twenty years of guilt. She knew it was more than the accident that brought Father James to the bridge on Christmas morning, but she saw in his eyes and heard in his voice the heartache the accident caused. She saw a man who was unable to forgive himself for a mistake made decades earlier.

As Elizabeth sat beside Father James, her hand resting gently on his, she felt a profound connection to the grief and turmoil swirling within him. The weight of his confession hung heavy in the air, a reminder of the burdens that souls sometimes carry in silence. She could sense the layers of his anguish, each one steeped in two decades of suppressed emotion and unresolved guilt. The depth of his sorrow deepened the new connection between them as it resonated with her own experiences of loss.

They sat in quiet reflection for a few minutes. Father James was grappling with a mixture of relief and fear. Relief that he had finally given voice to the burden he had carried silently for so many years, but also fear of the implications now that his secret was shared. Part of him felt lighter. Speaking about Jess and sharing the truth seemed to loosen the chains of guilt that had constricted his heart for so long.

Profound sadness permeated his thoughts. He mourned for Jess and the life she never got to live, a life he felt he had stolen in his moment of negligence. He thought about her parents losing a child and her brothers losing a sister.

"She'd be 37 by now," he said, breaking the silence. "Older than I was then."

"Thank you for telling me," Elizabeth said, trying to reassure him that sharing the story would help. "Jess sounds like she was a remarkable young woman, and I'm sorry you've felt this burden for so long."

"For twenty years, I've sat in that old car at the same intersection a million times in my head," he said, his voice catching. "I tell myself to keep my eyes open. Watch the light. Stay awake. See the truck. Keep Jess safe."

He started to cough.

"Sorry," he said through another cough.

She pulled an unopened water bottle from her bag and handed it to him. He caught his breath and seemed to be alright.

"This darn cough," he said dejectedly. "It's lingered for months now. I just can't shake it."

After a moment, Father James settled back against the pew, his breath steadying. The pause gave him a moment to gather his thoughts, a necessary break before delving back into the past. It was clear the memories were as vivid as the day they occurred, each recollection a fragment of a life-altering series of events.

He turned to look at Elizabeth, his eyes reflecting a deep-seated sadness mixed with gratitude for her attentive presence.

"Thank you for listening," he said, acknowledging the comfort her attention offered.

Reassured by her nod, he began to tell Elizabeth about the aftermath of the accident, his voice a mix of pain and catharsis. Sitting there in the pew felt like he was in his personal confessional. What he'd held in for decades, he continued to share with Elizabeth, each word unburdening his soul further.

***

Father James was discharged from the hospital the following day. He left with a freshly stitched laceration on his forehead, a mild concussion, and without a single broken bone. He returned to the rectory to recuperate and isolate. Parishioners volunteered to make him meals that were often left untouched, sitting on trays in the hallway outside of his bedroom.

In the solitude of his room, Father James grappled with a relentless tide of emotional anguish. The space around him, meant for rest and recovery, was more like a cell, trapping him inside with constant flashbacks, regrets, and feelings of hopelessness.

Every time James closed his eyes, he saw the truck, heard the screeching tires, and felt the impact all over again. He couldn't escape the thought that it was his fault. If only he had been more alert and more careful. The guilt gnawed at him, a constant, insidious presence that kept him awake at night. Only sleep and a strict regimen of round-the-clock painkillers could even try to mute the pain.

With each day that passed, the solitude forced Father James to confront the raw edges of his emotions. He wrestled with questions of faith and purpose, the 'whys' and 'what ifs' haunting his quieter moments.

He woke up on Friday morning dehydrated, hungry, and dazed. The trays of mostly untouched meals were swapped with those filled with fresh meals that would also go mostly uneaten. Still in a bit of a fog from the painkillers, he heard more noise than usual for a Friday morning outside the rectory, which sat on the lawn adjacent to the church.

He summoned enough strength to stand up and shuffle over to his second-floor window. His heart, already broken, somehow shattered again. There, in front of the church, sat a black hearse in front of a single black limousine. What seemed like hundreds of people, all clad in black, filed into the church's lobby as a line of cars still tried to make the turn into the parish's parking lot.

He stood at his window, holding onto the wall for support, in silence.

Minutes later, with the lot out of spots, people began parking on the rectory lawn. Their cars, crushing the recently fallen, brilliant fall leaves below, quickly filled the lawn as more opted to park on the side of the street.

There was a gentle knock on his bedroom door.

"Father, are you awake?" he heard the familiar voice of Ann Lombardi ask from the hallway. "Father James?"

He didn't know what to do. He hadn't spoken to anyone in days, but Ann had been a constant in his life since he arrived at the parish.

"I'm awake," he answered, his quiet voice sounding very groggy.

"I think you should be there today, Father," she said directly. "I can't force you, but I think you'll regret not going. Let me help you over there."

The thought of leaving his room hadn't crossed his mind, but now it terrified him. The church would be filled with mourners who were still in shock. He imagined the looks on the faces of her family. He thought about how the contrast between his face, still black and blue with a bandage across his forehead, and her casket, would illustrate how lucky he had been. He closed his eyes as his survivor's guilt resumed swirling again in his head. He knew he couldn't face Jess's family or the congregation.

"Father James," Ann called again from outside the room. "Please let me help you."

He paused, looked back out his window, and took a deep breath. He was terrified but knew he owed it to Jess.

"Alright," he said.

He walked to his bedroom door and slowly opened it. Ann stood there with the most compassionate smile he'd ever seen. Well into her seventies, Ann was short with poofed-up, bright white hair. She was like the parish's grandmother. She walked straight toward him and wrapped him gently in a hug.

"I'm here," she said. "I won't leave your side."

Within fifteen minutes, Father James took a quick shower and got dressed. He told Ann that he didn't want to be a distraction for the Taylor family, and they decided that he'd sit on the second level in the back of the church. The area was generally used for storage or to operate a spotlight during the annual children's Christmas play. Today, it would allow him to remain completely out of sight but still be present for Jess.

Ann pulled her car up to the rectory garage and drove Father James to the back of the school that connected to the church. There, he could walk in and get to his secluded seating area. They took their seats unnoticed and looked down on the packed church below. The nave was flanked on both sides by a kaleidoscope of colors coming from the stained-glass windows. The beams of the warm, wooden ceiling arched to a skylight that hung over the altar. A larger-than-life crucifix hung from the stone wall that served as the altar's backdrop. In their line of sight from the typically unused second level were the ceiling-mounted lanterns that hung over the congregants and provided soft, peaceful lighting.

Moments later, the piano began to play, and the cantor began to sing.

I, the Lord of sea and sky, I have heard my people cry, all who dwell in dark and sin, My hand will save.

Father Brendan, Deacon Stephen, and two altar servers began the procession. The two altar servers were brothers who attended the school attached to the church where Father James spent much of his time. Jack, an eighth grader with bright red hair, began processing toward the altar with the crucifix in his hands. His younger brother, Aidan, a fifth grader with brown hair, processed solemnly behind his brother. The pallbearers, a group of uncles and cousins, surrounded the casket and rolled it slowly on the downward-sloping center aisle. Finally, Tom and Linda

Taylor, with their sons Justin and Jason held tightly next to them, began the most challenging walk of their lives.

Here I am, Lord. Is It I, Lord? I have heard you calling in the night. I will go, Lord, if you lead me. I will hold your people in my heart.

Father James put his head in his hands and hunched over in his chair. His breathing became quick and panicked. He began to weep, his mind churning with turbulent thoughts. The solemn procession unfolding before him brought a sharp focus to his own internal turmoil. Every note of the hymn that filled the church, every step the pallbearers took, seemed to echo in the recesses of his soul, stirring up a storm of guilt and regret.

Ann pulled her chair closer and reached into her bag. She came prepared with tissues and a bottle of water in her purse. She handed them to Father James and began to gently rub his back.

"I'm right here," she said in a loving, grandmotherly tone. "You are not alone."

After the readings concluded, Father Brendan walked purposefully to the lectern to share his homily with his flock. Standing solemnly at the pulpit, he cleared his throat gently before beginning. The church, filled with Jess's family and friends, fell silent, each person bracing for the words that would offer solace and perhaps a bit of understanding.

"In times of grief," he started, "we come together not just to mourn but to celebrate the bonds that hold us as a community. Today, we gather not only in sorrow but in gratitude for the ties that bind us to one another and to God."

He paused, allowing his words to resonate with the congregation, each member reflecting on their loss.

"In Scripture," he continued, "we are told 'Blessed are those who mourn, for they will be comforted.' This comfort comes from our faith, yes, but it also flows from the love and support we offer each other in times like these."

Father Brendan looked around at the gathered faces, some tear-streaked, others stoic, all united in their collective grief. He saw Jess's parents holding their sons tightly.

"Jess's life, though short, was a testament to the love and joy she brought into this world," he continued. "She was a light in our community, a beacon of kindness and grace. Her spirit lives on in the memories we share, in the laughter she inspired, and in the love she gave so freely. In her memory, let us commit to living our lives with the same kindness and compassion that Jess showed every day. Let us support one another, lift each other up, and find comfort in knowing that she is with God, watching over us."

He let the silence hang for a moment, giving space for the congregation to absorb his message before concluding with a prayer, his voice a comforting balm in the stillness of the church.

"Lord, grant us the strength to bear our sorrows with grace, to support one another with love, and to continue the good works of those who have gone before us, in Your name and for Your glory."

As he sat down, Justin Taylor climbed the two stairs up to the altar and approached the lectern to begin the impossible task of eulogizing his twin sister. Justin paused for a moment and looked up to scan the scene in front of him. With his left hand clutching the edge of the lectern, he adjusted the microphone. The deep breath he took to calm himself echoed through the microphone and across the church.

He started by telling lighthearted stories about growing up with a twin and co-conspirator in childhood mischief to ease himself into his tribute.

"Jess had a laugh that could light up a room and a presence that felt like a warm embrace," he continued. "She dreamed big—of glamorous fashion runways in New York, of launching her own clothing line. But more than anything, she dreamed of making the world a little brighter, a little bolder."

Justin's voice wavered slightly as he continued.

"Her energy was boundless, and her compassion was profound. She believed in the goodness of people, and she acted every day to bring that goodness to the surface. She taught me so much about love and life, about fighting for your dreams, and holding onto hope even when the odds seem insurmountable."

He paused, his gaze lowering to the notes he'd barely glanced at, his next words coming straight from the heart.

"To imagine a world without her laughter and without her endless optimism is an impossible task."

Justin looked up again, undeterred by the tears sliding down his face.

"Today, we are tasked with saying goodbye to Jess, but let us also vow to carry forward her legacy. Let us be a little kinder, laugh a little louder, and love a little stronger, as she did. Let's do this not just to honor her memory but because it is what she would have done."

He closed his eyes briefly, then continued.

"Jess, you were my other half, my better half in many ways. I promise to live not just for myself but for both of us now. I love you, forever and always."

Justin's poise, maturity, and courage were on display for everyone to see. As it seemed like he was wrapping up his eulogy, he said that he wanted to say a few words about forgiveness.

"I pray that Father James is recovering from the accident," he said. "Let him know that we love him."

At the mention of his name, Father James immediately felt Ann squeeze his hand as his heart started racing again.

"Let none of us ever forget that this tragedy was an accident," Justin continued. "I look forward to telling Father James to his face that I forgive him."

Those words echoed in Father James's mind. The idea that Justin could forgive him so publicly just days after losing his sister and that he could find it in his heart to offer such compassion was both humbling and heartbreaking. Though he truly appreciated the sentiment, he was horrified to be mentioned by name. He wanted to disappear. His mind raced throughout the rest of the Mass, and he couldn't focus on another word said. Then, hearing familiar notes from the piano below, he stood up to leave as the cantor began the final hymn. As he looked down one last time, he watched as the casket was rolled back up the center aisle.

You who dwell in the shelter of the Lord, who abide in His shadow for life, say to the Lord, "my refuge, my rock, in whom I trust."

Father James and Ann made their way back down the steps toward the school the way they had entered to avoid being seen as the congregation continued to sing in a somber tone.

And He will raise you up on eagle's wings. Bear you on the breath of dawn. Make you to shine like the sun, and hold you in the palm of His hand.

They continued down the school's hallway when Father James stopped suddenly and turned to his left. The cafeteria, where the dance was held just six days earlier, stood in front of him, empty, dark, and quiet. Ann grabbed his arm and led him outside to her car.

On the drive to the cemetery, Ann took a circuitous route to avoid the intersection where the accident had occurred. Father James noticed and quietly appreciated the gesture. She spoke about the beautiful homily and eulogy, but Father

James just stared out the window, his gaze fixed on the world passing by his window.

As they entered Resurrection Cemetery, Ann drove away from the line of cars parking near the burial plot to avoid being spotted by the Taylor family. The towering crucifix at the entrance was surrounded by the cemetery's perfectly landscaped grounds. Father James and Ann sat in silence for forty-five minutes as the private interment took place a few hundred feet away. As they waited, the finality of it all began to settle in. When the last of the cars and the family's limousine pulled away, Ann started the car.

"No," Father James said. "I'll walk."

He stepped out of the car and began walking at a slow, deliberate pace as he watched his feet most of the time, avoiding the inevitable. As he approached, the two cemetery workers who were preparing to complete the interment walked away, recognizing a man in mourning who needed space.

As he arrived at the burial plot, Father James felt a tightness in his chest as he braced himself to say goodbye, to lay to rest not just a beloved member of his flock but also a part of himself that he knew would never fully recover.

Just before him sat her mahogany casket covered in dozens of yellow roses, her favorite flower. Father James fell to his knees and placed his hands on the top of the casket, knocking a few roses down. His hands trembled slightly as he touched the cool surface of the wood, each rose petal a vibrant reminder of Jess's youthful vitality and the beauty she had brought into the world. He prayed quietly as his tears landed on the ground below. Finally, he stood up. He fixed the flowers to look just right and took a step back.

"Please forgive me, sweet Jess," he whispered toward the casket, "because I'll never forgive myself."

***

Father James noticed how much time he and Elizabeth had been sitting in the chapel and knew the Midshipmen had strict rules about being out too late.

"You should get back to your dorm before lights out," he said, quickly standing.

He looked around to gather his things while avoiding eye contact with Elizabeth. He was glad he had finally shared the story, but he still felt shame for what happened to Jess two decades earlier. She gently grabbed his arm until he looked at her. They spoke with their eyes for a moment before she gave him a hug.

Elizabeth, having just heard the full weight of Father James's past and the burden of guilt he carried for decades, felt a deep empathy and concern for him. As he hurriedly suggested she return to her dorm, she noticed his discomfort and the way he busied himself to avoid her gaze, which spoke volumes about his lingering shame and vulnerability after sharing such a personal story.

[73]

"Excuse me," he said, pulling away from her embrace as he knew a coughing fit was imminent.

He turned and covered his cough with his sleeve. The cough, which he knew wasn't going away, was getting worse.

Elizabeth, who was collecting Father James's belongings, looked over and saw Father James, a dazed look on his face, staring at the unmistakable sight of ruby-red blood all over his sleeve. He looked up at her with a glazed expression on his face and abruptly reached out to grab anything with his hand to steady himself. Another cough came, and more blood followed. Before he could gather himself, his eyes closed, and he collapsed onto the floor, hitting his head on the side of the pew beside him.

The haunting sound of his body thudding against the church's hard floor echoed in Elizabeth's ears and in the empty chapel. She dropped what she was holding, the items clattering noisily beside her, forgotten in her rush to reach him. Now, on her knees over his unresponsive body, she shouted for help as she scrambled to find her phone to dial 911. Each ring of the phone seemed to stretch longer than possible as she begged silently for a quick answer.

Waiting for the paramedics, Elizabeth's hands shook as she knelt beside Father James, her eyes scanning his face for any sign of consciousness. She put her right hand on his head and prayed. Her other hand pressed lightly against his chest to feel the rise and fall. Each breath he took was a small reassurance.

For what felt like an interminable time, she waited alone for the paramedics to arrive. She glanced from his bloody head and shirt up toward the Winged Angel of Peace, looking down on him.

5

The Hospital

As Father James's eyelids fluttered open, a burst of disorienting lights and the wail of sirens greeted him, thrusting him into a reality he couldn't immediately comprehend. The discomfort of an oxygen mask against his face and the tightness of a harness across his chest added to his confusion. The ambulance's interior was a blur of white and metallic surfaces that swayed with the vehicle's swift movements. His eyes darted left and right, trying to piece together the fragments of his memory and understand how he had ended up strapped down in this frantic, flashing world.

Moving around the back of the vehicle, two paramedics wearing light blue shirts and navy blue jackets with an Anne Arundel County Emergency Services patch stitched on their right sleeves moved with urgent precision. They checked his vital signs and spoke into a handheld radio. His eyes, dazed from his fall, continued searching for answers.

The paramedic closest to him was a thirty-something Hispanic man with his name, RAMIREZ, sewn into his jacket in white lettering. He held Father James's hand steady on his chest and placed a pulse oximeter on his right index finger. He waited a few seconds before calling out to his colleague.

"Taylor, call this in to AAMC," he said directly.

His colleague, a young woman who looked as if she couldn't be more than 20, grabbed the radio and called ahead to their destination: the emergency department at Anne Arundel Medical Center.

"Anne Arundel Medical Center, this is Medic 37," she calmly relayed to the emergency department. "We have a 54-year-old male patient en route. He is presenting with acute respiratory distress and a head wound from a fall. His vitals are BP 92 over 60, pulse is 123, respiration 34, pulse ox is 86. Labored breathing with bilateral rattling sounds. The patient is receiving high-flow oxygen with a bag valve mask and an IV. We are approximately five minutes out. Please advise on further instruction."

As a woman's voice came through the radio to confirm the information, the young paramedic turned to assist her colleague. Father James looked up as she approached. He saw a pretty young woman with blonde hair under an Anne Arundel County EMS baseball cap. His eyes shifted to her jacket. He felt a surge of emotions overtake him when he saw her last name stitched on her jacket: TAYLOR. He closed his eyes as a wave of guilt overtook him, thinking about the pain he'd caused Jess and the entire Taylor family years earlier.

His heart, already strained under physical distress, now pounded with a heavy, almost unbearable emotional weight. He closed his eyes tightly, but a few tears escaped. Thinking he was just scared about his health, she grabbed his hand and spoke calmly.

"We'll be at the hospital in just a few minutes," she said to reassure him. "Don't worry. They're going to take good care of you, Father."

Taylor squeezed his hand but couldn't understand the significance of her presence to the priest lying in front of her. His heartbeat sped up as flashbacks blanketed his thoughts: the dance, the scream, the truck, the yellow roses. He wondered if he was hallucinating. His mind spiraled, and his heart raced. It wouldn't be the first time he'd seen Jess since the accident. From the altar, at a restaurant, sitting on a bench on the grounds of the Maryland State Capitol, he'd seen teenagers and young women who bore such a resemblance to Jess that his heart fluttered.

Now, only a week after being saved on the bridge, he was flat on his back and hooked up to monitors in a speeding ambulance, thinking about the worst day of his life—a thought that might be his last.

"Father, I need you to try to remain calm," Taylor said, seeing his vitals worsening. "We're not supposed to do this," she whispered to him, "but I'd like to pray with you."

She placed her hands on top of his, looked into his frightened eyes, and began to whisper.

"Heavenly Father, please watch over your son who needs you at this moment. Guide the hands of his doctors and keep him safe. Amen."

"One minute, Taylor," Ramirez shouted.

"Stay strong, Father," she whispered to him as the ambulance arrived in the bay at the back of the emergency department. "I'll be praying for you."

The back of the ambulance swung open, and he saw Ramirez and Taylor hop out and grab the end of the bed where he lay. They pulled him out and began wheeling him into the emergency department, where a doctor and two nurses were waiting.

Just as she'd done over the radio, Taylor, walking behind the stretcher down a fluorescent-lit hallway to an open bed, recited the facts she knew about him and his condition. She updated them about the jump in his pulse in the final two minutes of their ride and mentioned her concern that the last oxygen reading indicated his oxygen level had fallen to 85 percent.

"Take care of him," she said to nobody in particular as a curtain closed in front of her.

A tall, lanky man in his mid-forties with strawberry-blond hair in blue scrubs walked straight toward the bed as he finished pulling blue medical gloves over his hands.

"I'm Dr. Ryan," he said directly. "Can you tell me what happened?"

"The blood," Father James said, looking down at his stained shirt. "I had a coughing fit, a bad one. I must have passed out and hit my head."

He flinched as a nurse applied an ice pack to the area of his forehead that hit the pew. It was the same spot where he'd worn a scar since the accident two decades earlier. Another nurse placed a plastic nasal cannula under his nostrils to provide supplemental oxygen.

"Alright, sir," Dr. Ryan said, quickly stopping himself and noticing the clerical collar. "Sorry, Father, we're going to run some tests to figure out why you're coughing up blood. With your pulse ox levels being as low as they are, I'd prepare to spend at least a night with us here."

Father James held up his hand as if to ensure the doctor didn't leave as he began coughing again.

"No tests," he said between coughs.

Dr. Ryan tried to interject and explain his plan, but Father James emphatically waved him off.

"I don't need any more tests to tell me what's wrong," he said with a resigned expression. "I was diagnosed with lung cancer last month at Hopkins."

"Abby," the doctor said, looking back at one of the nurses, "we'll need everything we can get from Johns Hopkins."

Father James rolled his eyes at nobody in particular. He knew it was pointless to pull up his records, but he didn't have the strength to tell anyone at the moment.

"The good news is that you're stable, and your oxygen level has increased since you arrived," Dr. Ryan said. "I'm going to admit you so we can make sure you're healthy enough to go home and resume your treatment at Hopkins."

As the doctor left the room, a nurse took more vital signs and asked the standard patient medical history questions. Then, for a few minutes, he was alone. His thoughts drifted from the chapel and the ambulance to the bridge and the accident. Finally, he landed on a topic he'd thought about a lot lately—his cancer. He'd smoked only a handful of cigars more than 30 years ago. His father was a heavy smoker, he hadn't seen him in decades.

Father James's gaze drifted across the impersonal features of the room—the clinical, emotionless walls, the single chair that stood empty by his bedside, the light that cast a harsh glow over everything. It was in this isolation that he felt the full weight of his solitude. As he lay there, scared and alone, he was terrified, thinking about how the cancer would continue ravaging his body and drain the life from him. It was a factor, he admitted to himself, that led him on a snowy Christmas morning to the Naval Academy Bridge. The idea of dying alone was frightening, but to draw it out seemed to be unnecessarily punitive. He had friends and colleagues but no family. His mother died a few years earlier, his father walked out decades earlier, and he, of course, had no wife or kids. The only person he'd ever confided in was a first-year Midshipman he'd met only last week. He looked around his makeshift room with curtains for walls, and he saw nobody. The small confines of the room made him feel claustrophobic, and the curtains felt like barriers boxing him into his solitude. Yet, it was here, in this small, sterile space, that Father James confronted the totality of his life—his faith, his failings, and his fears.

He pondered the divine promises he had preached so fervently from the pulpit of salvation and redemption. Yet, in the stark loneliness of his room, these promises felt distant in the face of daily reminders about the impending end of his own earthly journey.

His failings, too, haunted the quiet moments as they often did. Memories of missed opportunities and those hurt by his actions weighed heavily.

Alone with just his thoughts, his fear of facing his Creator, of accounting for every choice and every deed, loomed large. It was a reckoning he had always known would come, yet now that it approached, it seemed all the more daunting.

Father James was relieved when his nurse broke the momentum of his negative thoughts by checking in on him. Abby made sure he was comfortable and convinced him to eat and drink a little bit. Soon, Dr. Ryan pulled back the curtain and stepped in. His quick pace and directness had been replaced by a deliberate demeanor and a solemn expression.

"Father Adams," he said, pausing to clear his throat. "It's been a few months since you were seen by the oncology team at Hopkins, and there are no records of your treatment. What's going on?"

Father James took as deep a breath as he could and sighed. His eyes met Dr. Ryan's, and his expression did the talking for him.

"You're not in treatment?" Dr. Ryan said incredulously, sitting down next to the bedside. "Listen, I get it. A small cell lung cancer diagnosis is bad, but treatment can prolong your life. Hopkins has the latest treatment options that might…."

Father James again put his hand up to stop the doctor.

"I know," he said as if to comfort the doctor. "I was in a very dark place before the diagnosis and have been for a very long time. A few months ago, the thought of going through chemotherapy and radiation to live another six months didn't matter. After tonight, I wish I could go back and make a different decision, but I have to live with that."

Dr. Ryan looked at him with empathy and acknowledged that there wasn't anything more he could do for his patient's underlying condition.

"At least I don't have to live with it for long," Father James added.

Dr. Ryan appreciated the dark humor and smiled.

"I'm going to admit you tonight," the doctor reminded him. "In the morning, I'm going to have a social worker come see you to make sure we have a plan for taking care of you."

After the doctor and nurses were done checking vitals, asking questions, and running tests, Father James was alone again in his room. He closed his eyes and felt a peace he hadn't known in many years. He'd collapsed, been rushed to the hospital, and knew he probably had two, maybe three months to live, but there was a peace he hadn't known for a long time. Offloading the guilt and pain from the accident to Elizabeth and discussing his mortality with Dr. Ryan left him feeling lighter.

After he was moved from the emergency department to a private room, the commotion of the hospital quieted around him. Father James found himself enveloped in profound silence, punctuated only by the soft beeps and dimmed lights of the machines monitoring his vitals. He usually dreaded the silence, but tonight, he felt a stirring of something he hadn't felt in a long time—hope.

The chaos of his emotions in the wake of his diagnosis, the encounter with Elizabeth, and the catharsis of the pew in the chapel becoming his personal confessional began to coalesce into a clearer picture of what he wanted in the time he had left. He didn't want his final weeks or months to be a countdown to the inevitable. Instead, he felt a newfound resolve take root within him to find peace and resolve old conflicts.

The next morning, after a surprisingly restful night, he was woken by a hospital social worker named Megan. She had shoulder-length blonde hair, reassuring green eyes, and a kind smile. He admired that she chose a career focused on helping people every day despite the meager pay.

Megan moved a chair to the side of Father James's bed, her expression gentle as she prepared to discuss the details that lay ahead. As she sat down, she smiled and leaned slightly forward to bridge the space between them.

"Good morning, Father James," she began, her voice soft but clear. "I'm here to help you think through some of the decisions about your care as you face these challenging times. It's important to us that your wishes are respected every step of the way."

Father James nodded, appreciating the sincerity in her approach.

"I want to be clear," she continued. "Dr. Ryan wants me to help you through this because of your diagnosis, but we are not admitting you to hospice care at this time."

"The first piece of good news," Father James said with a smile.

"Let's start with the type of environment you'd like to be in," she continued, pulling out a list of questions. "Some people prefer to remain in the hospital, while others feel more comfortable at home. Do you have a preference?"

"Home," Father James said emphatically, almost not even letting her finish the question.

"That's completely understandable," Megan said, jotting down notes in his chart. "When the time comes, we can help you arrange for hospice care at home, where you will have professional support in a comfortable environment. What about visits from friends and your parishioners?"

"I would like that," he said confidently. "I don't have any family, but I always feel my best surrounded by people."

Megan continued down her checklist of questions before they just began chatting like old friends.

"He's right in here," a voice said, approaching his room at the end of the hallway on the second floor of the hospital.

Father James looked up and saw a nurse leading Elizabeth into the room. He smiled, not only to reassure her but because he was genuinely happy to see her. He was hoping that she hadn't worried too much about him.

"Father James," she said, hesitantly approaching, "how are you?"

"I'm feeling better," he said, not yet wanting to go into detail.

She smiled and took a step back, realizing that Father James had been in a conversation with someone from the hospital. Megan stood up to leave.

"I'm glad you have a visitor, Father," she said. "We'll talk again later before we get you ready to head home."

Megan turned to leave. As she walked past Elizabeth, she grabbed her arm and gently pulled her closer.

"Thank you for being here for him," she whispered. "It really helps."

Elizabeth walked toward the bed and took the recently vacated seat.

"I'm glad to see you doing so well," she said with relief. "I'm sorry I wasn't able to come last night."

"Don't worry," he said. "You got me here, and I'm grateful."

After some small talk, Father James asked Elizabeth about life at the Academy and the classes she was taking this semester, and he gave her a blunt and detailed description of his medical situation. Elizabeth sat silently and stoically as he outlined his prognosis and his decision to forego treatment. It wasn't a fear of death that nudged him toward the bridge on Christmas, he told her. It was how the illness would ravage his body that brought him to the edge of giving up. He was miserable and guilt-ridden. Now, with a terminal diagnosis, he admitted, he decided not to prolong his fate. He finished by telling her about his new perspective and hope for his remaining time. Elizabeth absorbed the news, and they sat in silence for a few minutes.

Elizabeth glanced around the room, searching for something to say.

"I've been thinking a lot about our conversation on the bridge," she said, breaking the silence. "It's strange how people's paths can cross in the most unexpected ways."

"I don't think it was a coincidence," Father James said. "I believe it was a lifeline from God."

"It's funny," Elizabeth replied. "I never thought I would connect like this with a priest. I mean, I've always gone to church, but it's different when you actually talk to someone about real things and get to know them as a person, not just as a priest."

"I can understand that," he replied with a smile. "It can be easy to see priests as these distant figures. But we're just people trying to navigate life like everyone else."

They continued talking, sharing stories about their lives and about their shared passion for service, Father James to the Catholic Church and Elizabeth to the military. Elizabeth found herself opening up more than she had expected and embraced the budding friendship as they found more things they had in common.

"Can I ask you something?" Father James asked, his tone indicating a serious question was forthcoming.

Elizabeth nodded.

"You said you were running from something, and coming to the Academy was a needed change of scenery," he said. "What are you running from?"

Elizabeth paused and took a few deep breaths. She knew so much, including his most closely guarded secrets, about the man she'd met just a week and a half ago. Now, she knew it was her turn to share.

She shifted in her chair and looked out the window for a minute to collect herself. As she turned back, he could see the first signs of tears in her eyes. She took another deep breath, her face and body filled with resolve to reciprocate and share her guilt, deep fear, and feelings of vulnerability.

Taking another deep breath, Elizabeth felt transported back home almost two years earlier.

***

Rain began to fall from the overcast sky. Elizabeth and her best friend Kylie were running and laughing across their high school parking lot, trying to stay dry. Elizabeth, typically home immediately after school, stayed late to finish editing that week's edition of the school newspaper. She was taking over the role of editor-in-chief in the fall when her senior year began, so she decided to learn as much as she could from the soon-to-be graduates, with just a month left in the school year.

The girls paused to catch their breath after getting inside Kylie's green Jeep. The two had been inseparable since before they could walk. Growing up on neighboring farms in rural Grand Isle County and being born just one day apart was the perfect recipe for becoming best friends. They both dreamed of going to the same college, either Cornell or Penn State, to study animal science and agriculture before returning to take over their family farms one day. Elizabeth's recent success in cross country was complicating their plans as colleges began recruiting her from around the country.

Kylie, ever the chatterbox, filled the Jeep with stories from her day, her voice a familiar and cheerful sound that contrasted with the dull thud of raindrops landing on the roof. Their laughter rose above the noise of the storm, a buoyant sound that made the dreary day seem lighter.

The car pulled up to the farmhouse, and Elizabeth grabbed her backpack and ran inside to avoid getting even more soaked. Home later than usual, she knew she had to get right to work on her farm chores. At this point, she'd need to hurry to get to the milking parlor on time for the second milking of the day. She ran inside, got changed, and started hustling out of the front door of the only house she'd ever lived in. The old brick farmhouse, with a beautiful wrap-around porch, sat on 250 acres of land just a short walk away from the barn where they housed their Holsteins. Elizabeth and her brother Caleb, who was one year older, would become the fifth generation of Fitzgeralds to own and operate the farm when she took over for her parents.

Usually, the quickest way to the parlor was to go around the barn, but she decided to cut through to avoid the pouring rain. Elizabeth jogged down the path from the house and turned into the barn. She heard the rain drumming loudly on the roof, a chaotic symphony that drowned out the sound of her own footsteps. But as she stepped under the shelter of the barn, the world seemed to fall silent for a moment—

everything except for the scene in front of her. All at once, Elizabeth's heart began to race, her stomach sank, and a wave of nausea and dizziness overcame her. She felt like her legs might give out from underneath her from the weight of the shock.

Elizabeth's mind reeled as her eyes took in the scene. Time seemed to slow. Each second brought its own new wave of unbearable pain as she stood frozen at the entrance to the barn.

"No!" Elizabeth finally managed to scream.

It was a primal yell that could only be mustered under the most extraordinary circumstances.

Just thirty or forty feet ahead, her older brother Caleb lay motionless in the middle of the barn. Blood was splattered everywhere, and a pool of blood surrounded his head. For an instant, her eyes darted to the handgun just a few feet away from Caleb.

"Help!" Elizabeth yelled as she ran toward her brother.

She fell to her knees on top of his lifeless body and unleashed guttural noises of disbelief. She shook Caleb as if she was going to somehow undo the damage of the bullet. Her entire body, covered in her brother's blood, collapsed on top of him. One of the farm workers, who had just parked his truck outside the barn, came running after hearing her screams, pulled her off Caleb, and carried her out of the barn. For a moment, she sat motionless on the muddy gravel path as the rain poured down on her. Suddenly, her body flung forward as her stomach emptied onto the ground.

The farm worker tried to comfort her, but his words were lost in the confusion of the moment. Elizabeth's mind was a whirlwind of emotions, memories, and shattered dreams. Her heart managed to break over and over again with each passing second as tears poured from her eyes. Flashes of Caleb smiling went through her mind, his distinct laugh echoing in her ears. Now, all of that was gone in an instant. She tried waking herself up in case she was having a nightmare, but the increasingly chaotic scene around her, as more people showed up at the barn, made it clear this was her new reality.

***

Hearing Elizabeth's tragic story, Father James felt his chest tighten as his vision was clouded with moisture. As Elizabeth recounted the visceral details of her tragic loss, he felt immense sorrow for the pain and shock that she, still so young, had endured. His heart ached as he visualized the young woman before him, rain-soaked and crumpled over her brother's body.

Elizabeth steadied her breathing and grabbed a tissue from Father James's bedside table before continuing.

"Caleb had everything," she said. "He was smart, athletic, and popular. He was headed to Cornell in the fall to play football."

She paused and shifted again in her chair.

"Underneath, he was waging a war nobody knew about," she continued. "He left a note with details about the demons he faced, but that just made me question how I'd missed it. There had to be signs that were invisible to me. What if I'd known? What if I could have gotten him help? How could my own brother be in such a dark place without me knowing? The guilt was, and is, unbearable at times. I kept thinking I should've seen the signs, should've been there for him somehow."

Elizabeth stopped, tears still streaking down her cheeks, a stark reminder of the pain she carried. Father James felt a surge of compassion for the young woman before him.

"I completely shut down after I lost Caleb," she added. "I spent a few days alone in my room, and I barely said a word to anyone for some time."

"You know, Elizabeth," he began softly, "I know all too well about the 'what ifs' of life and how they can haunt us. But you were so young. Your brother cloaked his personal battles with his fun personality and success in life. Clearly, nobody saw any signs of struggle or depression. I hope sharing your pain with me today can have the same positive effect I felt sharing my story about Jess with you."

Elizabeth's admission hung heavily in the air, a testament to the pain and resilience etched deep into her being. Father James recognized the gravity of the moment.

Elizabeth wiped her tears, looking at Father James. His words, though simple, resonated deeply with her.

"The only way I found I could deal with the pain was by running," she continued. "Running became my escape, my way of coping with the pain and the guilt. I ran until the physical pain drowned out the emotions. Eventually, it became more than just an escape; it turned into my passion. I'm only here at Navy because of my running. Running has been my sanctuary. Every step, every breath, feels like I'm moving forward, even if it's just for a moment. It's when I feel closest to him, to Caleb. Like I'm carrying him with me, not as a weight, but as a reminder to keep going, no matter how hard it gets."

They sat in silence for a minute, the story weighing heavily in the room.

"When I saw you on the bridge," she continued, "I saw the signs I missed with Caleb. I knew I couldn't walk away."

Father James leaned forward, his eyes reflecting a mix of sorrow and admiration. For a moment, he felt like he was a priest again, consoling a parishioner.

"You've found a way to turn your pain into your strength," he said, trying to reciprocate the compassion she'd shown him. "That's not just coping; that's transforming your grief into something meaningful."

Their eyes met, and an unspoken understanding passed between them. In their shared vulnerabilities, they found common ground, a mutual respect that transcended the walls of the hospital room.

"Elizabeth, I want you to promise me something," Father James said, in an earnest tone. "Keep running, but not just for escape. Run towards something—towards healing, towards hope. I am here for you if you need me."

"It's a deal, Father," she replied. "But you have to keep moving forward too."

A few moments later, Elizabeth, trying to break through the seriousness of their conversation, unzipped the backpack she had brought with her and pulled out a small chessboard.

"Do you play?" she asked, a hint of curiosity breaking through the heaviness of their earlier conversation.

Father James's eyes lit up.

"I do," he replied with a smile. "It's been ages since I had a good game."

"You're on," Elizabeth said, returning his smile.

He pulled his food tray up to his bed and set up the pieces. As they moved the pieces, they talked about everything from books and movies to sports and family. As they played, Elizabeth felt a genuine connection forming. They both enjoyed bonding over far less serious topics. It was comforting to speak so freely with someone who, despite his own trials, radiated such calm and understanding.

As the game ended with Elizabeth shouting "checkmate" a little too loudly for being in a crowded hospital, she returned the conversation to a more serious note.

"I've been meaning to ask," Elizabeth started cautiously. "You told me about how difficult the last twenty years were after the accident. I know you struggled, but you still moved on with your life enough to continue being a priest. How did you get to that place in your life?"

Father James nodded with a slight smile.

"That," he said, "was not easy."

6

The Aftermath

Father James couldn't sleep. The silence of the night had become his personal torture chamber. After lying in bed for hours considering his options, he knew a change was desperately needed. He got out of bed, determined to find that change. As he moved around his bedroom, the only sounds were his footsteps and the sound of his dresser drawers opening and closing. He silently paced back and forth between his worn and faded wooden dresser and the modest twin bed in the corner of his bedroom.

He meticulously and quietly filled his suitcase with clothes and toiletries. He didn't want to wake Father Brendan, whose room was across the hall. He put on jeans, an orange and blue Florida Gators T-shirt, and a crimson hooded sweatshirt that simply read PREP across the front. He had received it as a gift from a teen in his youth group who graduated from a nearby Catholic high school last spring. The silence in his room was only interrupted by the soft sound of his feet and the suitcase zipper that sealed the only parts of his life in New Jersey he was taking with him.

He looked at his watch. 6:13 a.m. He knew he had to move quickly. The taxi he called would be arriving shortly, and Father Brendan would wake up soon to prepare for the first Mass on this Sunday. Father James grabbed his bag and walked toward the door. He took one final look back at the room where he'd lived for the past two years one final time. The rosary he'd kept with him every day since his mother gifted it to him upon entering the seminary was on the small desk next to the door. He grabbed it and tucked it under his sweatshirt. Everything else could be replaced, he thought. It was time to go.

Father James opened his bedroom door and slowly tiptoed toward the stairs. He stepped carefully, knowing the precise location of every squeaky floorboard on the old staircase. He walked to the kitchen and placed a hastily handwritten letter for his soon-to-be former colleague on the table.

Dear Brendan,

I'm sorry.

I am completely broken. I don't know if I'll ever
recover. I know I won't be able to do that here.

My carelessness is the only reason Jess isn't here today,
and I'll never be able to live with that.

Thank you for welcoming me into your parish community and into your home. I'll never forget the kindness you showed me. Please pass my apologies and best wishes to the parish and school staff. I don't have it in me to offer proper goodbyes. My heart is shattered, my guilt is all-consuming, and my future looks bleak. Any and all prayers would be greatly welcomed and appreciated.

I wish I was stronger, but I'm not.

Thank you, and I'm sorry.

James

He propped the letter up against an empty flower vase that sat on the kitchen table and placed his cell phone next to it to sever any communication with those he was leaving behind.

Father James held onto the back of a kitchen chair, took a deep, calming breath, and walked outside to wait for the taxi. Soon, he saw the headlights of a car pulling into the parish parking lot and turning toward the rectory. His mind turned to the finality of this moment. There was no going back after the accident and his secretive, cowardly exit. He waved to the driver, who placed his bag in the trunk.

"Philadelphia airport, please," he told the driver.

He clicked his seatbelt as the taxi headed back toward the exit next to the church. It wasn't all bad, he thought to himself. This is where his life as a priest really began. The parish and school communities were special. He had incredible memories of working with the kids in the school and the youth group teens. He'd made friends and truly helped people in need. He'd celebrated marriages, baptisms, and confirmations. He helped people deal with their grief at funerals and visited the sick in the hospital. As the taxi pulled away, his positive feelings began to fade.

He knew life in the priesthood meant that he wouldn't spend the rest of his life at this parish. He'd move on, maybe a few times, and eventually lead a parish himself. He often thought about the fact that he could be sent anywhere at any time, and he was alright with that. Though it would be hard to move on, he always took solace in the fact that he could stay in touch and visit the people of his first parish. This was different. He could never have imagined sneaking out under the cover of darkness without a word to anyone. No final Mass. No going-away party. No hugging goodbye.

The taxi's rearview mirror framed fleeting glimpses of the church, school, and the community where he'd lived— a stark reminder of what he was leaving behind. Father James stared out the window, watching the landscape change as they approached Philadelphia. The move was a desperate bid for anonymity, for a fresh start away from the reminders of how he felt like a failure. He felt like a coward, which further fueled his guilt. He thought this was the only way he could survive. He needed time and space. That wasn't possible at the rectory or in the community.

The car reached the apex of the Walt Whitman Bridge as they crossed into Pennsylvania. To his left, he saw the recently closed and soon-to-be imploded Veterans Stadium, home to the Phillies and Eagles since 1971. The hulking concrete bowl, though outdated, was home to many memories for generations of sports fans. This was the place where Tug McGraw threw the final strike of the 1980 World Series to bring the Phillies their first championship and the field where the Eagles beat the Cowboys just three months later to advance to their first Super Bowl in franchise history. It was where families gathered on hot summer afternoons to watch a baseball game and where people braved the elements to watch their Eagles play on frozen Astroturf in the snow. That chapter in Philadelphia would now end with the 60,000-plus-seat stadium unceremoniously falling to the ground.

Just across the street from The Vet, as it was known in Philadelphia, Father James saw the newly opened football stadium and an almost completed baseball stadium that would start the next chapter of each team's history. Whether the memories of the new stadiums would be good or bad was unknown, but both teams knew it was time for them to move on.

The taxi took the ramp from I-95 South to the exit for airport departures at Philadelphia International Airport.

"What terminal are you headed to?" the driver asked.

"Oh, uh, you can just take me to the main US Air terminal," Father James, unprepared for the question, said.

"B or C?" the driver replied.

"Doesn't matter to me," Father James said, knowing that he didn't actually have a ticket for any flight.

The driver looked back at his passenger with confusion but pulled over in front of Terminal B near a sign for US Airways. The driver got out of the car and pulled the luggage out of the trunk before setting it upright on the curb.

"Thank you," Father James said, handing him payment and a generous tip for the early morning ride.

He walked through the automated doors and looked around. For a Sunday morning, the airport was crowded with people getting ready to travel to destinations around the world. He spotted a US Airways counter and got in line. After a few minutes, a friendly woman greeted him.

"I'd like to go to Gainesville, Florida," he said with uncertainty in his voice. "I don't have a ticket yet."

"I can help you with that," she replied with an almost too-perky voice for being so early in the morning.

She smiled as she typed into her computer. A few moments passed as the woman typed and stared at her screen.

"Let's see," she said, waiting for her options to appear in front of her. "I can get you on a flight to Atlanta that boards in 55 minutes. You should be able to get through security in plenty of time. From there, you'll have a two-hour layover before landing in Gainesville before 2 p.m. How's that, sir?"

He hesitated for a moment because he wasn't used to being called "sir," but there was no way she'd know he was a priest. He wondered if he'd have to get used to that as he continued to question whether he'd be able to keep his vocation.

"Yes," he finally said, looking down at the woman's name tag. "That will be fine. Thank you, Pamela."

"My pleasure, dear," she said with excitement. "What day will you be coming back home?"

Home. The word stuck with him for a moment. Once the plane took off, this wouldn't be home anymore. He also didn't intend to relocate back to Gainesville. He had no idea where home would be.

"Just a one-way ticket," he said.

"Keeping your options open," she replied. "Good idea."

Father James paid for his ticket, surrendered his luggage, and headed toward the security checkpoint.

Starting to fade from his lack of sleep and the early hour, Father James got a coffee with two creams and extra sugar, and he sat down at gate C-4 to wait for his flight to Atlanta. He held his coffee with two hands wrapped around the cup. He enjoyed the soothing warmth as he closed his eyes for what felt like a moment.

"We're going to begin boarding flight 4133 to Atlanta," the desk agent said over the speakers.

His eyes opened quickly, looked around to get his bearings, and took a sip of his now room-temperature coffee. He stood up, threw out the coffee, and walked over to the line forming to board the flight. He handed his boarding pass to the attendant, walked down the jet bridge, and found his seat, 26A, toward the back of the plane.

He settled into his seat and soon found himself gazing vacantly through the small oval window beside him at the ground crew buzzing around the aircraft. The mechanical hum of the engines ramping up gradually lulled him back into another unplanned, shallow nap, broken intermittently by the soft murmur of passengers and the flight attendants' routine announcements.

Father James was jarred awake as the plane began roaring down the runway and shuddered slightly as it started climbing into the sky. He looked out the window and watched one chapter of his life end as the skyline of Philadelphia shrank beneath him. He shut the cabin window and closed his eyes.

The rest of the trip was uneventful. He was in a fog as he made his way through Atlanta's massive airport to find his connecting flight. A few hours later, he landed in warm and sunny Gainesville on time. He hadn't been home in a few years, and despite the pain he felt, both physically and emotionally, there was a small part of him that recognized it was nice to be back. He could rest and recuperate away from the microscope he felt he was under back in New Jersey. He walked outside and got in a taxi with a Gators license plate cover.

"I need to go to Southwest 23rd Terrace between Archer Road and Williston Road," he told the driver, forgetting the name of the apartment complex at the moment.

The taxi pulled out of the airport and headed toward downtown Gainesville. He looked out of the window along the ride, taking note of every change since the last time he visited his hometown. About 15 minutes later, the taxi pulled into an apartment complex. They drove past the clubhouse, pool, and a small man-made pond before arriving at Building 7 in the back. He got his bag and walked up a flight of stairs to the first door on the left. The gold letters on the door read 706.

Suddenly, a new wave of dread and uncertainty washed over him. Thoughts shot rapidly through his mind. She didn't know about the accident. He'd have to relive it all again. Maybe he shouldn't have come here.

It was too late; he was already standing at the door, and he had nowhere else to go. He knocked three times and took a deep breath as he heard footsteps approaching. The door opened, and a woman in her early sixties with streaks of gray hair stood in the doorway with a shocked expression.

"Hi, Mom," he said in a matter-of-fact tone.

"Jimmy!" she shouted. "What are you doing here?"

She quickly wrapped her arms around him and squeezed him tight. He tried not to wince from the pain as he was still bruised from the accident. She pulled away suddenly and looked into his eyes.

"Is everything okay?" she asked as the excitement on her face quickly turned to confusion and concern.

"Let's go inside," he said, brushing right past her concern.

His mom held the door for him as they walked into the apartment. She went over to the couch, cleared away the laundry she'd been folding, and turned off the television. Tired from the long trip, Father James just wanted to decompress. He walked over to the refrigerator and grabbed a bottle of water. He smiled at the sea of magnets that filled his mother's fridge. She loved her magnets and got one from every place she visited. Some of them date back decades. His favorite was a custom magnet she first put up when he was a little boy living in a house on the other side of town. "Stick to your diet, Pat," it said. She always said it was her little reminder to make good eating choices, and it had just become a staple in her home. It always made him smile. He noticed that it was next to two magnets, one from Rome and the other from Vatican City, that he had sent her from a trip to Italy shortly after being ordained. He walked back into the living room and sighed as he fell onto the couch.

It wouldn't be easy, but he needed to tell his mom what happened over the last week. Father James took a long sip of water, the coolness was a slight relief in the midst of his swirling thoughts and the heat he was no longer acclimated to. He settled deeper into the couch, feeling the familiar comfort of home yet acutely aware of the discomfort brought by the reason for his unexpected visit.

His mother, Patricia, sat opposite him, her eyes filled with a mix of concern and maternal warmth.

"Jimmy, talk to me," she said. "What's going on? You look... troubled," she said softly, her voice a blend of worry and care.

Father James took a deep breath, gathering his thoughts.

"Mom, last week, there was an accident," he began, his voice wavering slightly. "It was right after a group dance. There was this incredible young lady, one of the leaders of the youth group who organized the dance."

His voice caught as he tried to find the courage to just say her name.

"This girl, Jess, died in the crash."

Patricia moved from her recliner to the couch to sit next to her son, whose eyes had welled up. She reached out and wrapped his hands in hers.

"Oh, sweetheart," she said, only the way a mother could, seeing her child in distress. "I'm so sorry."

They sat in silence for a minute, her hands still holding his. Suddenly, she looked right at him.

"Why didn't you call?" she asked, realizing his story didn't entirely add up.

"There's more," he said, looking down. "I was in the car with her. I was driving when we got hit by a truck."

Patricia's eyes opened wide at her son's shocking story.

"Jimmy," she said, her tone more like the one he remembered from his childhood. "Are you okay?"

"A mild concussion and a few bumps and bruises," he said to reassure her. "But it's all my fault. I killed her."

Patricia hugged her son, who began to weep. This time, he winced in pain from the hug. She eased up but didn't let go. She knew there was nothing she could say to ease his raw pain, so she just held him while he cried.

She knew her son, his strengths, and his vulnerabilities. Seeing him so broken, so visibly shaken by the weight of the accident, tore at her soul. Patricia thought about the agony he must be experiencing, not just physically but emotionally and spiritually. As a mother, she wished she could absorb his pain and take it upon herself to spare him any further suffering. She was also struck by a resolute sense of protectiveness. She understood that now was not the time to press for details, to probe into the depths of the accident that had clearly left such a devastating impact on him. It was enough to know he was hurting; the specifics could wait until he felt strong enough to revisit the traumatic events.

Her mind was also racing with questions about the future— how to support him through his recovery, how to help him heal not just his physical wounds but the unseen scars that the accident had inflicted. She contemplated the long road ahead, the patience and understanding her son would require, and the love she would need to provide unconditionally.

After a few minutes, she pulled away from him and put her hands on his cheeks. She stared directly into his eyes.

"I love you, Jimmy," she said forcefully, as if to ensure the message pierced through his grief. "What can I do?"

"I need to rest and get away from everything," he said.

"Yes," she said reassuringly. "You stay here as long as you need before heading back. I'm here for you."

"I'll never go back to the parish," he said dejectedly. "I can't see the people I'd become so close to over the last few years and look them in the eyes anymore. That chapter is closed. I don't know if I'll ever be able to move forward with my life, but I know I definitely won't be able to do that in New Jersey."

Patricia knew it wasn't time to push that topic. She stood up, collected herself, and walked to the unused second bedroom in her apartment.

"Just relax," she said, taking charge. "I'm going to set up the room for you and fix you something to eat."

Father James put his head back on the couch and wiped the tears from his face. He watched his mom scurry around the apartment trying to find clean sheets and pillows for him before closing his eyes for a few moments.

The same question kept playing on repeat in his head. He was a full-grown man. He was a priest. How did it come to this?

7

The Reservation

Father James stayed with his mom in Florida for more than five months. During a time of the year that would typically have been very busy for him as a priest, he spent much of his time taking solitary walks or reading in his room. He spent a quiet Christmas with his mom in the apartment without gifts or festive decorations.

The walks, he thought, were the best thing for him. He enjoyed the warmth of Florida winters compared to New Jersey. Some days, he took his book and sat on a lounge chair by the edge of the apartment complex's pool to escape the small confines he shared with his mom. He was always an avid reader, and he found that he could let his mind wander in the world of the characters and spend less time thinking about the tragedy from only months earlier. He appreciated his mom's effort to keep his mind busy with nearly daily games of chess and Scrabble, and he genuinely appreciated the unexpected time he got to spend with her.

At night, there was no escape. He struggled to fall asleep, and nightmares and flashbacks would wake him regularly. It wasn't uncommon for his mom to rush into his bedroom and find him screaming, flailing in his bed, and covered in sweat. He usually struggled to fall back asleep after these episodes, and the lack of rest would follow him throughout the next day. It was a vicious cycle.

Patricia suggested therapy, but her son refused. Though not a certified psychologist, Father James was usually the one lending an ear and bestowing life advice to others. He harbored a deep-seated resistance to therapy, which was rooted in guilt and a sense of not being worthy of the help. He viewed his struggles as a test of his faith, a spiritual burden that he was meant to carry alone. He also knew that therapy would lay bare the unresolved emotions that he wasn't ready to confront.

In late February, Patricia convinced him to talk to a priest at Saint Augustine's Church, his parish growing up. With limited exception, he'd been AWOL with the Church since he left his New Jersey rectory in a taxi back in October. Father Brendan somehow found his mom's address and wrote to him fairly regularly, but Father James never sent a reply. His superiors knew where he was, and they were giving him the time and space he needed to process what happened and recover. He knew, however, that their patience wouldn't last forever.

On March 7, with his mom by his side for support, Father James walked into a church for the first time since the funeral. During the priest's homily about that Sunday's Gospel reading from the Book of Matthew, he focused on forgiveness, a topic weighing on Father James since the accident. He re-read a pivotal passage to drive home his point.

If you forgive others their transgressions, your heavenly Father will forgive you. But if you do not forgive others, neither will your Father forgive your transgressions.

"These words are both comforting and sobering," the priest began. "They offer us a promise of divine forgiveness, yet they also remind us of the responsibility that comes with it. To be forgiven, we must forgive."

Father James felt restless in his pew listening to the homily. He thought about how much harder it was to forgive himself than to forgive someone else.

"Forgiveness is at the heart of the Christian message," the priest continued. "Jesus himself, in his earthly ministry, exemplified this through his actions and teachings. Even on the cross, he prayed for those who crucified him, saying, 'Father, forgive them, for they do not know what they are doing.' When we forgive, we reflect the very nature of God."

The message was picking at Father James's fresh wounds. He tried to tune out the rest of the homily and went through the motions throughout the rest of Mass. Afterward, Father James and his mom stayed to meet with the priest. He waited for each of the parishioners who wanted a moment of the priest's time to finish and head home. Finally, the congregants filed out, and he approached the priest. He introduced himself and asked to chat. Father Terrence, the longtime pastor of Saint Augustine's, invited him to the rectory, where Father James shared the details of his last few months.

Father James heard some of the same themes he'd heard over and over: it was an accident, you need to forgive yourself, you need to live your life. He knew everyone else was right, but he didn't feel strong enough to forgive himself. Father Terrence, sensing he'd make little progress talking about self-forgiveness or offering pity, focused on Father James finding a purpose greater than himself. Before becoming a parish priest in Gainesville, Father Terrence had also served as a military chaplain during the Vietnam War. He spoke about how the soldiers did more for the person next to them than they did for themselves. His message paralleled his mom's message at the beginning of his final year of college.

Beyond platitudes and comforting ideas, Father Terrence had a tangible suggestion. He asked Father James to join a group of students from the University of Florida, which was directly across the street, who were going on a service trip in April during their spring break. The students would travel to the Navajo Nation in northeastern Arizona to do projects in support of Saint Michael Indian School. They'd spend their days alternating between manual labor and tutoring the students who ranged from preschool to twelfth grade. For Father James, he said, it would be a way to slowly transition back into his work and to serve others—to rediscover his purpose.

At first, Father James was unsure about the trip. He loved working with young people, but his most recent experience was tragically seared in his mind. He wasn't sure if he could contribute positively after everything that happened in New Jersey. Yet, the alternative—remaining trapped in isolation and self-reproach—was becoming increasingly unbearable. He couldn't spend the rest of his life living in his mom's small apartment. Something, he thought, had to change.

Seeing it as a potential lifeline, he agreed to join the trip. For the first time since the accident, he felt a tiny spark in his life. It was the first thing he was looking forward to since the dance marathon. Patricia was thrilled that her son was finally getting back to his life, even if it was only a small step.

On April 2, Patricia drove her son to Gainesville Regional Airport. After an emotional embrace, Father James walked into the terminal and left behind another place he had called home, but this time, he wasn't running away. Instead, he felt like he was moving toward something. He hoped his time in Arizona would reinvigorate his passion for service and working with young people. He prayed it would be the catalyst he needed to begin healing his wounds.

Along with Father Terrence and six students from the university, Father James boarded a small aircraft headed toward Atlanta, where they'd connect to a larger jet en route to Albuquerque. As the group from Saint Augustine's Church took off, Father James pressed his face slightly against the cool airplane window, watching the familiar landscapes of Gainesville grow smaller below. He saw the 157-foot Century Tower and nearly 87,000-seat Ben Hill Griffin Stadium on the University of Florida campus shrink beneath him. The hum of the engine blended with the low murmur of conversations among the university students accompanying him. Their youthful energy was palpable, filled with excitement and the occasional burst of laughter—a stark contrast to the heaviness he carried within. After a four-hour layover in Atlanta and a three-hour flight to Albuquerque, the group landed in New Mexico. Still, a two-and-a-half hour van ride awaited them before they arrived in St. Michaels, Arizona, just four miles from the New Mexico border.

When the group arrived after an exhausting day of travel, they were greeted by Sister Katherine, the school's principal. Only in her mid-forties, she stood tall with long black hair and kind brown eyes. She wore a turquoise rosary around her neck and walked quickly toward the group.

"I am so excited to see all of you!" Sister Katherine said excitedly. "Our community is so grateful that you've come to help us."

After meeting each of her guests, she showed the students to the two trailers they'd be housed in and walked Father James and Father Terrence to the rectory. After everyone settled into their temporary homes, Sister Katherine brought the visitors to some picnic tables outside of the school for dinner. They ate traditional Navajo food—mutton, squash, and freshly made Navajo fry bread. The students introduced themselves and asked questions about their upcoming work over dinner with Sister Katherine. As the evening went on, they marveled at the crystal-clear sky and the silence of the night. Hundreds of brilliant stars seemed to glimmer against the jet-black sky. The group, exhausted from their travels, went to bed early to prepare for their early wake-up call the next morning. The visiting priests stayed back a little longer to chat with Sister Katherine more candidly about the week ahead at her school.

"The kids are excited to have you here," Sister Katherine told them. "But, there is one student you should be aware of—Notah Nez. He's been here since preschool and is now in his final year of high school. The young man has been through so much, and he is on a path headed straight to jail or the morgue."

"Drugs?" asked Father James.

"Drugs, alcohol, fighting, and a contempt for authority," Sister Katherine said as if she was only brushing the surface of the issues plaguing Notah. "His father was in jail from the time he was a toddler. He died in prison after being stabbed when Notah was just seven years old. His mother has struggled with addiction for years, and he has no interest in letting anyone help him. He's been passed around between family members and has deep abandonment issues. I just wanted you both to be aware so nothing he does surprises you while you're with us this week."

Father James listened as Sister Katherine detailed the troubled history of Notah. Instead of intimidation or fear, he felt a sense of duty. He viewed this information not as a deterrent but as a call to action—a way to recommit himself to his pastoral duties. His instinct as a priest was to reach those who seemed furthest away and to extend his hand where others might withdraw.

After dinner and a pleasant conversation with their host, the priests returned to the rectory next to the school to rest before the beginning of a busy week. Father James felt a building sense of purpose he had lost months earlier.

Father James awoke the next morning as the first rays of dawn crept over the horizon, painting the vast Navajo sky with hues of orange and pink, in a world profoundly different from anything he had known. The quiet of the morning was broken only by the distant sound of farm animals. It was a moment of peace, a stark contrast to the turmoil within him.

After breakfast with Sister Katherine and Father Terrence, Father James met with his group from the university for a briefing on the day's tasks. Father James listened intently as Sister Katherine outlined the week's projects: repairing a fence around the school's playground, painting the school's main hallway, and setting up a new computer lab using funds the students raised from the Saint Augustine's community in the months before the trip. But what caught his attention most was the tutoring program for students who needed extra help. He remembered Father Terrence's words about finding purpose and wondered if this might be a step in that direction.

As the group dispersed to start their day, some went to find supplies, and others went to the classrooms to assist the teachers. Father James spent the morning with a small group of first-grade children, reading stories and laughing with the kids. He read three books from the well-worn collection of *Sweet Pickles* book series from the 1970s in the classroom library. Though the books were worn and often held together with tape, the kids loved the stories featuring the lovable animals who were always getting into hijinks in the *Sweet Pickles* neighborhood. The kids laughed as he did silly voices for each character and struggled to keep them all straight.

Father James ate his lunch in Sister Katherine's office and spoke quickly and excitedly about his morning. Interacting with the students, helping people in need, and feeling he had a purpose, energized him. She didn't know firsthand who Father James was before the accident or how it had affected him, but she was thrilled to see his enthusiasm for his work at her school. He felt like a new man.

"You've seen the best we have in our school, the innocent, eager learners," she said with a smile. "Are you ready for a challenge?"

"The young man you mentioned last night?" he asked, his excited tone surprising Sister Katherine.

Sister Katherine's eyes widened as she nodded.

"I'd love to see what I can do," he replied.

At 1:15 each day, Notah Nez was required to visit the guidance counselor. These meetings were just one part of an agreement between the school and his mother to avoid expulsion. Father James went to the counselor's office and waited. Though he promised Sister Katherine he wouldn't fill himself with unrealistic hopes and expectations, Father James was excited to meet Notah. After checking his watch a few times, he finally saw Notah approach the office at 1:23 p.m. The young man, in wrinkled khakis and a halfway tucked-in white polo shirt, walked in, dropped his bag on the floor, and sank into the couch.

"Notah, this is Father James," the counselor said. "He's visiting from Florida as part of the service group here this week."

Father James took a step forward and extended his right hand. Notah looked away, avoiding eye contact with the stranger standing in front of him. Father James ignored the slight and pulled his chair closer to the couch.

"Today, you'll spend this period with Father James," the counselor said before leaving her office.

Notah's piercing brown eyes narrowed with a mix of suspicion and defiance as he scanned his surroundings. If he stood up straight, Notah would eclipse six feet, with broad shoulders, visible muscles, and calloused hands. His long black hair was unkempt, and he was at least a few days past when he should have shaved his patchwork facial hair. He carried himself in a way that showed his hardened and impregnable exterior and made sure you knew he didn't want to be wherever he was.

"Why don't you tell me about yourself," Father James said, hoping this wasn't going to be as difficult as it seemed.

Notah smirked and didn't respond. He looked surprised that the visiting priest didn't seem to know his reputation. Father James took a minute to evaluate his options. Clearly, pleasantries and small talk were nonstarters, and he didn't have time to build a rapport before heading back to Gainesville. It would be uncomfortable, but he decided to try to penetrate Notah's defenses with shock. If he could just start a conversation, any conversation, maybe he could break through Notah's barriers.

"I hear you're a tough kid," he started. "You don't want to talk to me. That's fine. I get it. But don't think for a second that this is going to bother me."

Notah rolled his eyes. He'd heard it all before. Years of teachers and counselors had tried to break through to him, and he'd mastered how to ensure their efforts were as short-lived as possible.

"I don't know you or what you've been through in life," Father James continued. "But you don't know the shit I've dealt with either, kid."

Rather than roll his eyes, Notah actually glanced over at Father James, probably just out of surprise at the choice of language. Father James, desperate to break through and make a difference, figured he could at least try to get his attention by doing the unexpected. He composed himself before talking about the day he never brought up intentionally. He looked directly into Notah's eyes so that he knew his words would be heard.

"The last teen I worked with before coming to the reservation died in a car crash that was my fault," he said. "Trust me. Your attitude won't bother me."

Nobody at the school, certainly no priest or nun, had ever spoken to him like this before, and he was naturally curious about the car crash, especially given how bluntly Father James mentioned it.

"Huh?" Notah grunted, stunned at the admission.

Father James took a deep breath and smiled widely on the inside. He was so uncomfortable speaking so casually about the accident, but he hoped it would spark a conversation. It worked. He told Notah about his time in New Jersey, the accident, and how he ended up in Florida and now the reservation.

It wasn't a dialogue, but the young man was listening.

"So, you ran away," Notah said.

"As fast as I could," Father James admitted.

He saw his own vulnerabilities, insecurities, and guilt as a way to turn him from a random visiting priest to another person living with trauma.

"I don't know you, Notah," Father James said, trying to break through to the young man. "I'm not judging you or pretending to understand what you've dealt with or where you've come from. I am, however, present. I will listen, and I won't act like I know everything."

They sat quietly together for a minute. Father James saw more contemplation and less contempt in Notah's demeanor. The bell rang for the end of the period, and Notah grabbed his bag, stood up, and walked toward the door.

"I hope we can talk tomorrow," Father James said.

Notah looked right at Father James before his eyes quickly glanced away. He left without a word, but he didn't dismiss the idea. The meeting could have gone a lot worse, Father James thought.

Father James regrouped with Sister Katherine after school and told her about the meeting with Notah. Once again, she urged caution and explained how a long list of priests, nuns, teachers, counselors, neighbors, therapists, and psychiatrists had tried to work with him. Father James acknowledged the difficult task but still held onto the hope that he could make a positive impact.

Back in the rectory after dinner, Father James's mind focused on his work at the school, the joy he got from reading to the younger kids, and the nearly impossible task he'd taken on with Notah and not on the accident. That night, there were no nightmares, and he didn't wake up suddenly in a pool of sweat. He woke up a few minutes before his alarm was set to ring, fully rested for the first time in six months, and he had an excited energy as he got ready for his second day at the school.

That morning, he started his day in a fifth-grade classroom, assisting Mrs. Natani. Trying to instill a love of reading in the children, she turned to the incredibly popular *Harry Potter* book series. Each morning, before her language arts lesson, she spent about 15 minutes reading from the series. Father James, a big fan of the books himself, excitedly volunteered to read Chapter 12 – The Polyjuice Potion in *Harry Potter and the Chamber of Secrets*. For those fifteen minutes, he read aloud to the class with excitement and made up his own funny voices for each character as Harry Potter and Ron Weasley traversed the halls of Hogwarts looking like Crabbe and Goyle due to the polyjuice potion they'd cooked up in Moaning Myrtle's bathroom. The students hung on every one of JK Rowling's words and roared with laughter when the story revealed how the potion went terribly wrong, and Hermione Granger ended up transforming into a cat.

He remembered going to the local Borders Books in New Jersey almost a year ago when the fifth book in the series, *Harry Potter and the Order of the Phoenix*, was released. Now, he was thrilled to use the fantastical world filled with broomsticks, wands, and moving staircases to nurture what he hoped would be a lifelong love of reading in these children.

After reading to the fifth grade, he worked with a small group of second graders who needed extra help with fractions, and he finished his morning speaking to a high school religion class about his experience in the priesthood. They did not hang on to every word like the fifth graders did with *Harry Potter*. Still, it had been a good morning, and he was looking forward to his afternoon meeting in the counselor's office. He ate his lunch and arrived early to go over Notah's mile-long disciplinary record and bleak transcript that shouted "social promotion." Just as the bell rang to start seventh period for the high school students, Notah walked in and assumed his familiar position on the couch.

"I was in a freshman religion class today talking about the priesthood," Father James started. "I gave them an overview and a high-level look at what led me to my vocation, but it wasn't the time or place to really get into what really drove me to where I am. Ultimately, my father is the biggest reason I wear the collar. He was verbally and emotionally abusive toward me, and he beat the hell out of my mom. There were a few times before I was old enough to have a driver's license that I had to drive her to the emergency room. It was brutal. Then, when I turned 18, he left, and I haven't heard from him since."

Notah was silent, but he was clearly listening.

"After he left, I stayed close to home for college to help support my mom," he continued. "I needed something positive in my life, and I started going to church and joined an intramural softball team with other students who volunteered at Saint Augustine's. I still remember the hot August morning on my first day of classes in my senior year at the University of Florida. I was eating breakfast, and my mom walked into the kitchen. 'This is it,' she said. 'Your last year of college. Go find something you love to do that makes a real difference in this world.' I thought about that advice for weeks. Meanwhile, I was spending all of my free time either at church, playing softball with friends from church, or volunteering for community service opportunities led by the church. One day, it just hit me. Maybe the priesthood is the answer to my mom's challenge. I like to think that any time I help someone in my capacity as a priest, it helps make right some of the horrible things my father did to us. Somehow, him being an awful person led me to try to help others—like you."

"Who the hell do you think you are?" Notah asked defiantly. "You're just wasting your time. Everyone else has tried to help me and eventually gave up. Go pick some other helpless kid to save."

"Maybe I am wasting my time," Father James retorted. "Maybe this is the best version of you. Maybe you're content with a bleak future. But how about I decide how I spend or waste my time?"

Notah looked surprised to hear such blunt commentary from a priest, especially one who didn't know him.

"If I am wasting my time," Father James continued, "then that's all I'm wasting—time. But you're wasting something much more valuable—your life."

Notah only rolled his eyes and ignored him.

"I know people have tried to scare you straight and tell you the path you're on leads to jail or a cemetery. They're not wrong, but let's think less about the path you're on and more about the one you could be on. I'm not going to BS you into thinking that if you just study harder you'll be off to the University of Arizona in the fall. For now, that life is not a reality. Maybe that life isn't ever going to be for you, and maybe it will. Who knows? But what if you graduated from here and joined a group of young people where your family life, report card, or past mistakes don't matter? What if you were a part of a group of people who truly looked out for each other like a family?"

"Yeah, that sounds great, Father," Notah shot back sarcastically. "But there's no way I'm gonna be a priest. But, you can tell whoever you need to that you tried really hard."

As Father James laughed, Notah looked puzzled.

"The priesthood?" Father James asked incredulously before shifting to a more serious tone. "No, I want you to think about joining the military."

Notah's skepticism was evident, but for the first time, a flicker of curiosity shone in his eyes. Father James recognized this as a small but significant breakthrough.

"The military," he explained, "isn't about escaping your past. It's about building a future. It's about discipline, yes, but also about belonging to something bigger than yourself. It's about purpose."

Father James paused, allowing his words to sink in.

"Think of it, Notah. The military could be a place where your strengths are honed, where you're valued for who you are and what you can become, not just judged for your past mistakes. Take my mom's advice. Make a real difference in this world. I'm sure you've learned about the Navajo Code Talkers and the incredible impact they made during World War II. You can continue their remarkable legacy."

Notah, silent and confused at first, slightly relaxed his defensive posture as if he was giving the idea real thought.

"You want me running around in the sand and killing people in Afghanistan or Iraq?" he asked.

"I want you to find a family," Father James said. "I want you to be a part of something bigger than yourself. I want you to set up the rest of your life."

Notah nodded but again remained silent. The idea was planted, an alternative narrative to the one he had been living. The bell rang, and Father James didn't push the idea further; he knew some seeds needed time to germinate.

Disappointment set in for Father James on Wednesday and Thursday when Notah was absent from school. He worried that he had pushed too hard, and now Notah was keeping his distance. He vented his feelings to Sister Katherine, but she had her own theory. Notah often missed school because he was taking care of his mother, who might have overdosed or been taken to the hospital to have her stomach pumped after a night of binge drinking. Father James stood silently in Sister Katherine's office, imagining everything Notah had and would continue to go through if nothing changed drastically in his life.

"This kid needs to get off the reservation," Father James said bluntly. "He'll never survive here."

On Friday, at 1:15 p.m., Notah walked into the counselor's office. It was the last school day the volunteers from Florida would be on the reservation before their trip back to Gainesville in the morning.

"Are you alright?" Father James asked, concerned after Notah's unexplained two-day absence.

"Fine," Notah answered dismissively, his tone hinting at a setback rather than a breakthrough.

"I've been thinking about our conversation a lot over the last couple of days," Father James said. "Have you given my suggestion any more thought?"

"Not really," Notah said unenthusiastically. "But don't worry, you can go home back to Florida and tell everyone you made a real difference here on the reservation. You swoop in for a few days, tell me how to fix my life, and now leave. I'll figure my own life out."

Notah grabbed his bag and left the room. Father James scurried to the door, but he didn't know what to say. All the hope he felt for Notah evaporated in an instant. He spent the rest of seventh period alone in the office, thinking about what he could have done better. Now, with the end of the trip looming, it was too late.

Father James stood motionless at the door, his hand still resting on the frame long after Notah had disappeared down the hallway. The sting of Notah's words cut deeply, leaving him feeling a mixture of frustration, sadness, and an acute sense of inadequacy. He had come to the reservation with high hopes. He thought he could make a meaningful impact and rediscover his purpose, yet the dismissal in Notah's voice echoed loudly, challenging the very core of his intentions.

Father James's heart felt heavy, weighed down by a sudden, crushing realization of his own limitations. He wondered if he could have approached their conversations differently, if he had misread his pupil, or if there was a sign he failed to see. These thoughts churned inside him, feeding a growing sense of helplessness. The stark reality that his efforts might not have even scratched the surface of Notah's deep-seated troubles was disheartening. He realized that his expectation to make a genuine difference in Notah's life in such a short time was unrealistic, but it didn't blunt the disappointment.

The following day, Sister Katherine hosted the group for a send-off breakfast. The students told stories about their work over the last week and the memories they'd take with them back to Florida. By a quarter to nine, it was time for them to get in their van and head back to Albuquerque to catch their flight back east. Sister Katherine gave everyone a hug and handed out cards some of the younger kids had made for their new friends. As the students loaded their duffle bags and backpacks into the car, Father James walked over to have a private conversation with Sister Katherine. They spoke for just a few minutes before he walked over toward Father Terrence and the group.

"You all know my story," Father James said. "You know how I came to be in Florida and why I'm on this trip. I want to thank you all for welcoming me and being a part of my healing journey. Coming to the reservation with you was the best thing that could have happened to me at this point in my life."

The group nodded along, but most weren't sure why Father James was addressing the group.

"But my work here isn't done, and I have no parish or school or job to go back to in Gainesville. I've talked to Sister Katherine, and until I'm given a new assignment, I'm going to stay here and try to make a real difference for this incredible community."

Announcing his decision to stay at the reservation felt like stepping into a new chapter of his life, one that was both daunting and deeply necessary. He glanced around at the surprised faces of the students and volunteers, each a witness to the transformative journey he had embarked upon.

As he looked into Sister Katherine's supportive eyes, Father James felt a much-needed affirmation of his decision. Staying on the reservation was not just about healing himself but about giving back, about investing his energies into a community that could benefit from his presence as much as he could from theirs. The warmth of the community's reception and the genuine connections he had begun to forge bolstered his resolve.

The students all came over to give Father James a hug goodbye. Last to greet him was Father Terrence.

"I'm really proud of you, Jim," he said. "You're going to make a real difference here."

The group got in the van and began driving away. Father James took a moment and looked around. He was standing on the Navajo Reservation in a rural town in Arizona. Only one word came to mind—home.

8

The Field Trip

Father James paced back and forth from the school office to the front door, waiting. None of the students, and only a few teachers, had arrived. Then, as he stepped outside, he saw Notah slowly walking up to the door to the high school wing of the school building. He looked like he'd woken up just minutes earlier.

"Why did I have to get to school so early today?" Notah asked Father James as he walked up to the door just after 7 a.m. on Thursday morning.

"We're going on a field trip," Father James replied with a twinkle in his eye. "Just the two of us."

After not returning to Florida a few weeks ago, he built up enough credibility with Notah to begin developing a strong relationship. Declining the trip home was a pivotal moment, one that resonated deeply with Notah. Father James's decision to stay signaled to Notah that he wasn't just another adult making empty promises but someone who truly cared about his future. Father James made a point to be present every day, showing up early and staying late. He was always ready to lend an ear or offer guidance. Notah was initially guarded and skeptical of Father James's intentions. But as the days turned into weeks, Notah began to lower his defenses. They talked about everything—schoolwork, life on the reservation, and Notah's aspirations after graduation. Father James listened intently, never judging, always offering support and encouragement.

One day, after a particularly rough week, Notah found Father James waiting for him after school. In addition to their usual session in the office, Father James suggested taking a walk. They wandered around the school grounds, Father James sharing stories from his own troubles as a kid with an abusive father. He told him about how he confronted his father on his eighteenth birthday and used it as a turning point in his life. He pointed out the parallels in their lives— both had faced abandonment and hardship, but Father James had found a way to turn his pain into something meaningful. Now, he wanted the same for Notah.

In their talks, Notah mentioned that he'd barely left the Navajo Nation except for a few trips to nearby Gallup, New Mexico, to see the rodeo and a handful of trips more than a decade earlier to visit his dad at the Arizona State Prison Complex in Winslow, just two hours southwest of his home.

"What are you wearing?" Notah asked with a laugh, surprised Father James wasn't wearing his usual black shirt, matching pants, and a white collar around his neck.

"I don't always need to look like a priest," he said with a smile while sporting a T-shirt, shorts, and baseball hat.

Father James and Notah walked toward his car and got in. He looked to his right, seeing Notah buckling his seatbelt. A surge of anxiety, almost like a rush of adrenaline, coursed through his body. The last time he drove a student was Jess. In an instant, he saw the truck and heard her scream. He saw the doctor stitching his wounded forehead, the casket in front of the altar, and the yellow roses. He worried that he'd taken on too much and wondered if he was ready.

"Where to, Father?" Notah asked, breaking the spiral of thoughts racing through his mind.

His head shook subtly as if he was getting rid of the negative thoughts and coming back to reality.

"You'll see," he said with a smile. "It's going to be a long day though."

Shortly after they left the school, Father James pointed the car southwest on I-40.

"This is the way I went when I visited my dad in jail," he said casually as he stared out the window at the same scenery he remembered as a young child, thinking about those uncomfortable visits.

"You'll take a different path," Father James said with confidence. "You've had a tough childhood, but your future isn't written. It's your choices now that will set you up to write your own story."

Notah listened to every word but didn't reply. He just stared out the window. Soon after passing the entrance to Petrified Forest National Park, home to magnificent and colorful petrified wood, they saw a sign with an arrow pointing to the right for ASPC – Winslow, the prison where Notah's dad spent his final years. Instead, Father James turned onto Route 377 under the sign that read 'PHOENIX – 180 Miles'.

"Are we going to Phoenix?" Notah asked.

"This field trip is about showing you the world out there for you beyond the reservation," Father James said. "You already know about life in the Navajo Nation, but you don't know anything else. We're going to change that today."

The vast desert landscape was spread out as far as they could see on the two-lane road. After a while, they saw a few mobile home parks with tall pine trees. Father James looked over at Notah and found that his companion had fallen asleep. He smiled, looked back to the road, and kept moving.

As he continued driving toward the state capitol, he couldn't help but think about the weight of the responsibility he felt toward Notah. The young man had faced so much hardship, more than any teenager should ever have to endure. He thought about the undeniable parallels he saw between Notah and himself. They had both been abandoned by their fathers in different ways, suffered devastating losses, and had times when they struggled to find their place in the world. Father James felt a deep connection to Notah, a kindred spirit of sorts, and a burning desire to help guide him toward a better future.

Father James thought back to his own journey, the choices he had made, and the paths he had taken. He remembered the feelings of isolation and hopelessness that had once consumed him and how those experiences had ultimately led him to the reservation. Now, he knew, it was time to take the lessons from his life and use them to help the teenager asleep next to him. Today, he hoped that by exposing Notah to new experiences, he could help him see that his past did not have to define his future.

After a few hours, Notah sat up abruptly, his eyes adjusting to the bright sunlight pouring into the car. They had already entered Phoenix, and Notah was taking note of his unfamiliar surroundings.

"What the hell is that?" he shouted, suddenly ducking in his seat.

A Southwest Airlines plane roared just a few hundred feet over their car as they headed north on I-10. The blue Boeing 737, with its red undercarriage and tricolor tail, was landing just to their right at Phoenix Sky Harbor International Airport.

"It's fine," Father James said, comforting his frightened companion. "It's just landing at that airport."

"I've never seen a plane like that before," he said, shocked at both its size and his proximity to it. "Sometimes we see little planes going over the reservation, but that thing was huge."

Notah's eyes followed the plane until it touched down on the nearby runway. For the next few minutes, he craned his neck to get a look at each plane taking off and landing. Father James smiled at the boy-like innocence he saw from the eighteen-year-old sitting next to him. A few minutes later, he pulled the car into a parking garage and found a spot on the second level.

They emerged from the garage onto the sidewalk in downtown Phoenix, and Notah was shocked at the bustling city before him. His eyes widened in amazement. For the first time, he was face-to-face with the immense structure of Bank One Ballpark, home to the Arizona Diamondbacks. The stadium loomed before him, its massive, modern design unlike anything he had ever seen on the reservation. The exterior of the ballpark was a blend of red brick and glass, its sleek lines and towering walls reflecting the sunlight in a dazzling display. The sheer size of the stadium was overwhelming; it seemed to stretch endlessly in both directions, a monument to the world of professional sports and urban life. The curve at the top, a retractable roof, highlighted the cutting-edge technology with which he was unfamiliar.

[138]

"Ready to go see a ballgame?" Father James asked with a smile.

"We're going in there?" Notah asked with a look of disbelief, pointing at the massive ballpark towering over them.

"That's the plan," Father James replied. "I know it was a long drive, but I think we'll have a good time getting some food and watching the game."

As they approached, Father James took two tickets out of his pocket and handed one to Notah, who inspected every detail. They handed their tickets to the attendant at the entrance and walked onto the concourse toward the field. Notah's eyes were larger than ever as he stood at the back of section 120, looking at the field below. He was struck by the vastness of the scene before him. The green expanse of the baseball field stretched out like an emerald sea, perfectly manicured and pristine. The diamond, with its carefully drawn lines and gleaming bases, seemed almost surreal in its perfection. The enormity of the scoreboard towering above centerfield caught his eye next. The giant and vibrant display was filled with player statistics, colorful graphics, and a lot of advertisements. The scoreboard also showed the game's starting pitchers–Randy Johnson for the Diamondbacks and Vicente Padilla for the Phillies. Looking around the stadium, he felt a rush of excitement mixed with a sense of disbelief. Never in his life had he seen anything so grand, so full of life and energy. The sights, sounds, and smells of the ballpark were almost sensory overload, but he loved it.

Father James watched Notah's reaction with a smile. He could see the wonder in the young man's eyes, the spark of possibility that he had hoped to ignite. He brought Notah to Phoenix to show him that the world was vast and full of opportunities. He wanted the young man to see that there was so much more to see and experience beyond the borders of the Navajo Nation.

"This is incredible," Notah finally said, his voice barely a whisper as he continued to take in the sight of the stadium.

"The reservation is your home and an incredible place," Father James replied, placing a reassuring hand on Notah's shoulder. "But I just wanted you to see how much more there is out there for you to discover."

After a few minutes of taking in the grandeur of the ballpark, Father James and Notah began walking through the busy concourse. They bought hot dogs, popcorn, and sodas before heading to their seats in section 215 on the second deck along the third base line. From their seats, they could see the pool just behind the fence in right-center field, a unique element of the seven-year-old stadium.

After standing for the National Anthem, they listened to the public address announcer welcome the crowd to Military Appreciation Day. A man, who looked to be no older than 24 or 25, slowly walked toward the pitcher's mound. He wore the number 20 Diamondbacks jersey of 2001 World Series hero Luis Gonzalez and shorts showing his prosthetic right leg. The crowd roared with chants of U-S-A as Private First Class Daniel P. Kennedy threw the honorary first pitch to Gonzalez. Father James noticed how intently Notah was watching the scene unfold. He watched how the crowd admired the local military veteran and absorbed the sacrifice the soldier, just about seven years older than him, made for his country.

"Pretty incredible, right?" Father James asked.

Notah didn't say a word, but his eyes tracked Private Kennedy as he walked off the field to a rousing ovation.

They watched the first inning in silence, enjoying the atmosphere. The crack of the bat, the roar of the crowd, and the smell of the ballpark food filled the air.

"Did you see that play?" Notah asked as the crowd groaned at the spectacular play by the Phillies shortstop. "That was incredible."

"Yeah, that's Jimmy Rollins," Father James said, nodding in agreement with Notah's amazement with the play. "He makes plays like that all the time. I saw him play a few times when I lived near Philadelphia."

As the game went on, they chatted about the players, the strategies, and the different pitches. Notah was shocked at how fast Randy Johnson, the 40-year-old, towering lefty, could throw and the movement he had on his famous slider. Father James explained how he was one of the greatest pitchers in baseball history, having won the Cy Young

Award for the league's best pitcher five times already in his career.

After a few scoreless innings to start the game, Steve Finley smashed a home run to lead off the bottom of the fourth inning to right-center field near the pool. His home run gave the home team a lead and sent the crowd into a frenzy. Notah stood up but forgot to clap. He was transfixed by the crowd's frenzied reaction.

The Diamondbacks couldn't hold on as Johnson gave up a mammoth home run to all-star first baseman Jim Thome in the top of the seventh inning. The Phillies tallied two more after a pitching change and scored a fourth run in the next inning on a wild pitch. Phillies closer Billy Wagner had an easy bottom of the ninth to clinch the win for the visitors and send the crowd in Phoenix home with a loss.

As they made their way out of the stadium, Notah paused and looked back at the field one last time, soaking it in. Father James pulled a disposable camera out of his pocket and asked an usher to take their picture.

"This was awesome," he said, turning to Father James after their photo was taken. "Thank you."

"I'm glad you liked it," Father James replied.

They walked back to the car and began the long drive back to the reservation. As they drove away from the stadium, the car ride was filled with a comfortable silence for the first few minutes. Notah kept looking back at the ballpark, a grin on his face.

"That place was amazing," Notah finally said, breaking the silence. "I wasn't sure I'd ever even go this far from the reservation."

"You deserved a day like this," Father James replied, glancing over at Notah.

Shortly after leaving Phoenix and passing north of Mesa, the cityscape gave way to the familiar open desert. The sky was painted with the colors of the setting sun, casting long shadows over the landscape.

"So, what did you think of Randy Johnson?" Father James asked, trying to keep the conversation light.

"That dude is huge," Notah said, shaking his head in disbelief. "I've never seen anyone that tall before. And that slider, it's crazy how much he can make it move."

They casually chatted about their favorite parts of the game and how different Phoenix was from the reservation despite only being a few hours away. Then, sensing an opportunity, Father James used a break in the conversation to continue a discussion they'd had during their one-on-one sessions at school.

"I noticed how you were watching that young military veteran who threw out the first pitch," Father James said. "What were you thinking about?"

"It was impressive," Notah replied. "I liked the way the crowd respected him and the way he carried himself."

"I know we've talked a lot about your future," Father James continued. "I really think the military is perfect for you. Until recently, you were going down a bad path. The military would give you a purpose and open new possibilities for you. There's a whole world out there for you to explore. You saw a small part of it today. I want you to believe in yourself and take the opportunities that come your way."

Notah was silent for a moment, processing Father James's words.

"I've thought about it a lot since you first brought it up," he admitted. "But it's a big decision. I'm still not sure if it's the right path for me, but I haven't made up my mind."

"I understand," Father James said gently. "It's not a decision to be taken lightly. I just see so much potential in you, Notah. I know the military could help you channel that potential and provide you with opportunities you don't have right now."

Notah looked out the window, the vast desert becoming darker before him.

"It's hard to imagine," he said. "Growing up, I never thought I'd leave the reservation, and the military would take me to the other side of the world."

"Just think about it," Father James replied. "I'm so proud of everything you've done since we met. Let me know if there's anything I can do to help."

Notah nodded but didn't respond. They drove in silence for a while longer before Father James glanced over and found Notah asleep again.

A few hours later, Father James pulled into the familiar road leading to the reservation under a canopy of brilliant stars. He glanced over at Notah, still asleep, and felt a mix of hope and uncertainty about what the future held for him. The long day had been a lot for both of them, but he knew it was worth it.

As the car came to a stop in front of Notah's mobile home, he gently shook the young man awake. Notah blinked groggily, taking a moment to recognize where he was.

"We're home," Father James said quietly.

Notah rubbed his eyes and sat up, looking around. He seemed almost reluctant to leave the car, as if stepping out meant returning to reality after the surreal day he'd just experienced.

"Thanks for today, Father," Notah said, his voice still heavy with sleep.

"You're welcome, Notah. Get some rest, and we'll talk more soon."

Notah nodded and opened the car door, stepping out into the cool desert night. He gave Father James a small wave before heading inside. Father James watched him go, a feeling of cautious optimism settling over him. He knew there were no guarantees, but he felt today had been a step in the right direction.

As he drove back to the rectory, Father James couldn't help but think about the challenges that lay ahead for both of them. The weight of responsibility pressed down on him, but it was balanced by a reinvigorated sense of purpose. He had seen a spark in Notah's eyes today, a glimpse of what could be. That was enough to keep him going.

When he finally pulled up to the rectory, the night was quiet and still. He stepped out of the car, stretched his tired limbs, and made his way inside.

Exhausted, he ate a quick snack and got ready for bed. As he closed his eyes that night, Father James felt prepared to face whatever came next. The future was unknown, but for the first time in a long while, he felt ready to meet it head-on. He felt Notah was ready too.

9

The Knock

Father James beamed with pride as he took his seat on the gymnasium stage. He was suited head to toe in his faculty cap and gown, and he used the graduation program in his right hand as a fan. Just two months after arriving on the reservation, he sat in a packed gym on a hot, June evening. As the rest of the faculty walked down the center aisle toward the stage, he stopped fanning himself to read the program. He saw Dakota Lapahie's name listed as the class valedictorian. The incredibly impressive young lady was bound for Stanford University in the fall on a full academic scholarship to study medicine. She dreamed of returning to the reservation and opening a clinic.

Then, listed alphabetically, he saw the list of graduates in the high school class of 2004. Father James's finger moved quickly down the list until he reached the 'N' names. His lips tightened, his eyes welled, and he felt a surge of adrenaline when he saw the name he was searching for. Notah Nez.

Graduation was never a certainty for Notah. Between his barely passing grades and his ample disciplinary file, Notah was destined for a very dim future. The last two months, however, changed everything. His first few meetings with Father James and the idea of joining the military set him up for a breakthrough, but it wasn't enough. Feeling like Father James was just parachuting into his life for a week only to leave him behind heightened his issues with abandonment.

As he watched the graduating class process into the gym with broad, proud smiles, Father James thought back to the moment he surprised Notah in the guidance counselor's office. He had made the decision to stay on the reservation not just as a commitment to Notah but as a step toward his own healing. The idea of their mutual recovery was a driving force in his mind, a symbiotic journey where both could find redemption and strength. When Notah reluctantly strode into the counselor's office after that weekend, he was shocked and confused when he saw Father James sitting on the couch waiting for him.

"I stayed because I believe in you," Father James told him. "I stayed because I care about you."

Remaining on the reservation and staying with Notah was the recipe for finally tearing down the towering walls the young man had built around him for so many years. Soon, the unlikely pair became inseparable. Every effort he put into helping Notah navigate his challenges was also a step toward healing the scars left by his own past.

They'd meet every day in lieu of his old counseling sessions, and Notah began staying after school to get extra help from his teachers. Sister Katherine insisted she didn't throw the word "miracle" around casually, but it was the only word she could find to describe the sudden, likely lifesaving turnaround in her most challenging student.

After a passionate speech by Dakota, Ms. Yazzi, the school's assistant principal, began calling out the names of each graduate who walked across the stage to receive their diploma and a hug from Sister Katherine. Father James clapped for each student as he impatiently waited for them to work their way to the middle of the alphabet. Finally, the moment he waited for arrived. Notah stood at the foot of the stairs that led to the stage and made eye contact with Father James, whose eyes couldn't hold back the tears.

"Ladies and gentlemen," Ms. Yazzi started, breaking up the rhythm she'd set announcing each student's name. "To present our next graduate with his diploma is our favorite visiting priest, Father James Adams."

Surprised, Father James looked toward the podium where he saw Sister Katherine stepping back and waving to him to take her place. Encouraged by the faculty sitting around him, he stood up, walked to the center of the stage, and took the diploma from Sister Katherine.

"Alright, let's continue," Ms. Yazzi said with a smile and excitement in her voice. "Notah Nez."

Notah climbed the stairs and walked directly toward Father James. As he approached, Father James extended the diploma in his left hand. In that short moment, he thought back to the first day he met Notah, seeing a young man burdened by his circumstances and struggling against the weight of his past. Each interaction, each moment of resistance, and each breakthrough played through Father James's mind like a film reel. Notah didn't slow down or reach for the diploma. Instead, he went right in for a massive hug. His long arms fully wrapped around Father James, and he even pulled him off the ground a few inches. The pure joy of the moment was one Father James would never forget. After he was released from Notah's grasp, he wiped the tears from his eyes, handed the diploma to the young man, and posed for a picture as the audience roared with approval.

Father James walked back to his chair and couldn't focus on anything for the rest of the ceremony. He thought about what he gave up when he entered the priesthood. He knew he'd miss significant life moments like getting married or seeing the birth of a child. This, he swore to himself, would be one of those core memories that he'd hold onto for the rest of his life. This, he thought, was what he gained from his vocation.

When the ceremony ended, Father James offered his congratulations to and took pictures with scores of graduates and received congratulations from much of the faculty. After most of the attendees dispersed, he found Notah waiting for him just outside of the gym. He was standing and talking to a man wearing a formal Army dress uniform.

"I'm so proud of you, Notah," Father James said with a hug as he made his way outside. "I'm Father James," he said, offering his hand to the man in uniform.

"Sergeant Gambrills," the man said, shaking Father James's hand. "I'm an Army recruiter based in Gallup, New Mexico. I want to thank you for encouraging this young man to visit our office."

Father James looked over at Notah with a curious smile. They had talked many times about the idea, but he had no idea Notah had actually met with a recruiter. Only a few weeks earlier, after the baseball game, Notah said he wasn't sure if the military was the right place for him.

"I've thought about it a lot, Father," Notah added. "You are right. This is something I know I need to do, and I'm ready. I kept thinking back to seeing the veteran throw out the first pitch at the Diamondbacks game and the way the crowd respected him. I want that. I want to earn that."

Overcome with emotion, Father James stood stoically for a moment, holding back the tears forming in his eyes.

"The thing is," Notah continued, "I leave for Fort Sill, Oklahoma on Monday to begin 10 weeks of basic training."

Father James felt a swirl of new emotions as he stood before Notah and Sergeant Gambrills. Pride surged through him first, bright and clear, at the sight of Notah taking such a decisive step forward in his life. It was a path he had suggested, a chance for discipline and direction, yet seeing it come to fruition brought an unexpected tightness to his chest.

As Notah's words settled in the air, a sobering realization dawned on Father James. Notah was not just considering the military; he was committed, with departure imminent. The news jolted him, stirring a protective concern that shadowed his initial pride.

"Take good care of him," he said to Sergeant Gambrills. "He's a special kid. A special man."

He gave Notah a hug and held him tightly.

"I'm proud of you, son," he whispered.

Father James unwrapped his arms from Notah. He wasn't sure what his face must have looked like, as he was so confused by his wide range of emotions.

"Go enjoy the rest of your day," he said, breaking the emotional tension.

Over the weekend, Father James found himself caught in a reflective pause, a deep contemplation not just of Notah's future but of the paths they had both traversed. Sitting in the modest confines of the rectory, his profound sense of accomplishment mingled with a paternal concern. He worried about the dangers and hardships Notah would face but was simultaneously buoyed by the young man's courage to embrace such a transformative step. In the solitude of his room, he prayed for Notah's safety, his strength, and his continued growth.

On Monday morning, after a sleepless night, Father James found himself pacing outside the rectory as the first light of dawn broke over the horizon, casting a soft glow over the reservation. The air was crisp for now as another scorching June afternoon loomed.

Just after 7 a.m., he saw the headlights of a car pulling into the church parking lot. It pulled up to the rectory, its engine cutting through the quiet morning. Father James walked toward the car when he saw it was Notah in the driver's seat. Still dressed in civilian clothes with a duffel bag sitting on the passenger seat, he stepped out of the car and carried himself with a mix of determination and nervous anticipation.

"Father James," Notah called out, his voice steady but carrying an undercurrent of emotion.

Father James approached, noting the resolve in Notah's eyes—a far cry from the young man he had first met just a couple of months ago.

"Notah," Father James replied, his voice thick with emotion. "I was hoping to see you this morning."

"I couldn't leave without saying goodbye," Notah said. "You've done so much for me. I… I just wanted to thank you one more time."

The two stood in silence for a moment, the weight of their journey hanging in the air between them. Father James reached out, placing a hand on Notah's shoulder, feeling the maturity and strength that had emerged within his pupil.

"Notah, you've done the work," Father James said directly. "You've made the choices that have brought you here. I'm proud of you, not just for enlisting but for having the courage to take charge of your life and change your path."

Notah nodded, the hint of a smile tugging at the corners of his mouth.

"I'm going to make you proud, Father," he insisted. "I'm going to make something of myself."

"I know you will," Father James assured him, his heart swelling with a mixture of pride, hope, and sadness at the farewell.

With those words, Father James pulled Notah into a hug, a gesture that spoke volumes of the respect and bond that had formed between them. Notah turned toward the car that would take him to the beginning of his new life.

"Wait," Father James shouted, reaching his right hand into his pocket. "I want you to take this with you."

He reached out and handed Notah his rosary.

"This is my graduation gift to you," he continued. "My mom gave me this when I first enrolled at the seminary. I want you to take it with you to remind you that He's always with you."

[154]

Notah looked at it for a moment, taking in the importance of the gesture, before placing it around his neck and offering a final hug goodbye.

Watching Notah drive away, Father James felt a sense of peace. The reservation, which had been his place of refuge and healing, had also been the backdrop for a remarkable transformation—not just for Notah, but for himself as well. While he was focused on helping Notah find his way, Father James had rediscovered his sense of purpose and reaffirmed his own path.

As Notah's car disappeared from his view, Father James whispered a prayer for the young man's safety and success. Then, turning back to the rectory, he felt an invigorating sense of resolve that he hadn't known since the accident. He knew there were more Notahs out there, and his work on the reservation was far from over.

For the next few months, Father James thought about Notah frequently. He imagined him going through the rigor of basic training that could test his limits. He was confident that his pupil would succeed and grow as a man.

He also welcomed a new group of University of Florida students to the reservation. This time, the group spent four weeks doing manual labor and running a summer camp for kids from the reservation. Father James was so grateful for the support from the college students. He'd written to Father Terrence in Gainesville about Notah and included a note about how the camp was due to close early this summer due to a lack of volunteers.

The reinforcements, who brought orange and blue Gators gear for the kids to wear, made a measurable difference for the children they served. Instead of being on their own all day, a few dozen kids had activities, arts and crafts, games, and even a few field trips to fill their summer days.

Although the four weeks went quickly, the bonds they formed were strong. There were many tears shed by both the kids and the volunteers when it was time for them to return home to Florida.

For Father James, the end of the summer meant preparing for his new role at the school. Sister Katherine created a Swiss Army Knife-type job for him to best leverage his skills and experience. He would do some one-on-one and small group tutoring, assist the guidance counselor with students who were particularly difficult to reach, and support the campus ministry department with a focus on community service. From the moment he entered the seminary until the accident, he often wondered where he'd be called to serve. He imagined himself in many roles, but working on the Navajo Reservation in a lightly populated part of northeastern Arizona was never in the picture. Yet, this is where he felt at home and at peace after a tumultuous ten months.

On August 31, days before Labor Day weekend, Father James received a letter from Notah. He wrote about the difficulty of basic training and how he persevered. He mentioned loving the camaraderie in the Army and how he knew this was the right choice. At the end of the letter, he told Father James that he would soon be deployed to Afghanistan to support Operation Enduring Freedom. He couldn't give any more specifics, but he assured Father James that he was ready. Father James found an enclosed photo of Notah wearing fatigues with the rosary prominently placed around his neck.

The new school year got off to a promising start, and Father James felt truly a part of the school family for the first time. Father James enjoyed his new routine. Every morning, he positioned himself by the school's main entrance, ready to offer a cheerful word or some encouragement to the students as they came in. This small gesture made a big difference in setting a positive tone for the day. No longer a visitor, he was able to greet kids in the hallway by name, and his success with Notah had earned him some credibility with both students and faculty. By mid-September, he really hit his stride and began to see some encouraging progress with some of the students who needed the most support, both academically and emotionally. He felt at home in a place so unlike any he'd ever been before his trip with the volunteers from Florida.

Inside the classroom, he was more involved than ever. He worked closely with students who needed extra support, aligning with teachers to provide both academic and emotional assistance. His office became a known sanctuary for those looking to share their troubles or just find a quiet moment away from the school's hustle.

He called home to his mom every Saturday to check in and tell her about his week at school. He shared every success in such detail that she began to ask about certain students by name. Beyond the pride she felt hearing about the impact her son was having on the reservation, she was encouraged by his progress each week. She knew he would never truly stop grieving the loss of Jess, but there were times when he was living with her in Florida when Patricia worried her son would never be able to move forward with his life and return to any semblance of normalcy. Now, she saw her son healing. She was also planning her first visit to Arizona in October, which excited her son. He couldn't wait to show off the school, the reservation, and the people who had helped change his life.

After just the first month of the school year, the fruits of his labor were evident. Students who had struggled in the past were now making noticeable progress. Seeing these changes gave Father James a deep sense of fulfillment and confirmed that he had truly found his place within this community. He was proud of his work and the progress made by the students, but he was determined to do more.

On an early October Sunday morning, just days before his mother's scheduled visit, Father James was enjoying the quiet of his unassuming bedroom in the rectory. He leaned over his desk, engrossed in the plans he was developing for a new community service initiative that would create opportunities for students of all ages to give back and serve others. His mind was alive with his budding vision for a program he was calling FaithWorks, a term originally coined by his mentor at the seminary, Father John. The name was inspired by one of his favorite passages in the Bible that came, ironically enough, from chapter two in the Book of James.

Someone will say, "You have faith, and I have works." Show me your faith without your works, and I will show you my faith by my works...For as the body without the spirit is dead, so faith without works is dead also.

The core of FaithWorks would be its hands-on projects. Father James envisioned his students venturing out into the community where their youthful energy could be channeled into meaningful actions: beautifying parks, stocking shelves at local food banks, and sharing smiles with homebound seniors. These acts of service, he believed, would plant seeds of empathy and civic responsibility in the young minds.

To deepen the students' understanding of the program, Father James planned to weave FaithWorks into the school's curriculum. High school science classes could adopt nearby Ganado Lake, restoring it as they studied its ecosystem. History students could learn about the reservation's unique heritage and share their findings with the public.

He also envisioned a leadership component, particularly for the high school students. They would take the helm of planning and executing projects, mentoring their younger peers, and honing their leadership skills in a real-world context. This leadership track would not only empower the older students but also create a mentorship pipeline within the school.

His mind, racing with plans, was interrupted by a firm knock on his bedroom door. He stood and crossed the room with a sense of curiosity as he wasn't expecting a visitor. Opening the door, he was met with a sight that instantly filled him with dread. Sister Katherine stood before him, her usually composed demeanor undone by red-rimmed eyes and an expression filled with sorrow.

"Sister Katherine?" Father James's voice was laced with concern as he noticed her appearance. "What's wrong?"

The words weighed heavily on Sister Katherine as she met his gaze. The hallway, typically a place of passing greetings and light conversation, felt silent and heavy.

"It's Notah," she said, her voice barely above a whisper.

The name hung in the air between them for what felt like minutes as Father James felt his legs begin to lose their strength.

"Notah?" he echoed. His mind raced through a list of possibilities, each more unwelcome than the last.

"He was shot," Sister Katherine's voice cracked with the effort of delivering the news. "In Afghanistan. He's dead. There was a firefight, and he was trying to ...."

Father James didn't hear another word she said. The world around him seemed blurry, and the room felt like it was spinning. He grasped the door frame for support, but it didn't help. He fell to his knees in front of the grief-stricken nun.

This can't be happening again, he thought. Images flashed through his mind at a rapid speed. Jess smiling at the dance. The truck. The casket. The roses. Notah in the counselor's office. His graduation. Their goodbye outside the rectory. A casket draped with an American flag. The images played on a torturous loop in his head.

He threw up on the floor and on Sister Katherine's shoes, and his face fell to the floor and landed in a pool of vomit. He heard Sister Katherine screaming, but he couldn't make out what she was saying. His head felt like a spinning top, and he desperately and unsuccessfully tried to catch his breath.

"It's happening again," he said quietly to himself.

Sometime later – he wasn't sure if it was a minute or an hour—he was sitting on the edge of his bed with Sister Katherine. There was a glass of water in his hand, but he had no memory of how it got there.

"This can't be happening again," he said, this time aloud for Sister Katherine to hear. "Not again. I've killed another kid."

Sister Katherine tried comforting him, but he wasn't listening. It was as if the room went completely silent, and everyone else was moving in slow motion.

"I told him to join the military," he interrupted, suddenly feeling like he was moving at the speed of everyone else. "Another kid would be alive if it wasn't for me."

Notah, a young man whose life had just begun to turn a corner, whose future had brimmed with newfound purpose, was gone. The weight of the news and the ensuing guilt bore down on Father James with a suffocating force.

Father James had no concept of time, but at some point, a doctor whom Sister Katherine knew from Gallup, about 30 miles east, was in the room. He checked Father James's blood pressure, heart rate, and his breathing. With the priest's consent, he administered a sedative. A short while later, he was asleep.

The next morning, he woke up to find Sister Katherine asleep on a chair that was usually found in the living room of the rectory. She'd stayed with him all night and woke up at the sound of Father James sitting up in his bed. He looked to his right and made eye contact with the nun, but he lay back down and rolled over before she could say a word. Seeing that he still needed some time, Sister Katherine left the room but kept the door open so someone could hear if he needed anything. This was not the first time she had lost a student or a recent graduate, but this loss was especially difficult since she saw how Notah turned his life around and how it would haunt Father James.

A few hours later, Sister Katherine saw a white SUV pull up to the front of the school. Four people in their thirties and forties emerged wearing professional-looking cross-body bags. She walked quickly toward them and thanked them for coming so quickly. After hearing the news on Sunday, she made a few phone calls to ensure grief counselors were present for the next few days at school and in the community. She sent three of the counselors into the school's main entrance while she walked another toward the rectory.

Father James heard the footsteps approaching, followed by the squeak of the already ajar door.

"James," Sister Katherine said softly before taking a few steps into the bedroom while her companion stood by the door. "I need to talk to you."

He felt numb and generally disinterested in talking to anyone, but he couldn't say no to Sister Katherine—the woman who helped him tremendously the last time he was going through trauma. He took a prolonged and quiet breath in and exhaled before turning around and sitting up in his bed. He looked past the familiar face of Sister Katherine and at the stranger standing in the doorway. He was tall, with black hair and a graying beard. Clearly of Hispanic descent, he wore glasses and held a bag in his right hand.

"Father James, I'm Carlos Torres," he said. "I'm very sorry to meet you under these circumstances, but I'd like to offer you my support. I'm a grief counselor, and Sister Katherine brought me and three of my colleagues here from Phoenix to support the whole community through this tragedy."

Though he'd previously rejected the idea of therapy, Father James was in crisis and didn't want to make the same mistakes he had made after the accident a year earlier.

"What happened?" Father James asked bluntly. "I need to know what happened to Notah."

Carlos sat down in the chair Sister Katherine had used as a bed and leaned forward.

"The family has shared the initial report from the Army with me," Carlos told him. "I'll share with you what I have. It will be very difficult to hear, but it may help you on your road to finding closure."

Carlos pulled the report out of his bag, which he'd read in the car on the way to the school. He paraphrased some parts to massage and humanize some of the matter-of-fact writing that was filled with military jargon.

"Along with his unit, Private Nez was on a routine patrol in the Helmand Province in southern Afghanistan when they came under unexpected and fierce fire from enemy combatants," Carlos read aloud. "Private Nez utilized his training to move members of his unit to safety behind a rock formation near the road where they patrolled. There, Private Nez sent radio communications requesting backup and air support."

Carlos looked up to see how Father James was reacting to his words. He gave a consoling look and continued.

"Another member of his unit, a Private Dawkins, was struck by enemy fire about fifteen yards from where Private Nez had taken cover. Private Dawkins suffered significant injuries, but he remained alive. Private Nez instructed the members of the unit also taking cover behind the rocks to provide cover as he dashed toward his fellow soldier. He hooked his arms under the armpits of Private Dawkins and began dragging him toward the cover of the rocks. When he was about five feet from the safety of cover, Private Nez was fatally shot in the neck. Other soldiers in the unit moved quickly to drag Private Dawkins to safety and recover Private Nez's body. After air support arrived and eliminated the enemy, Private Dawkins was transported to a nearby medical unit. Private Dawkins survived his wounds and was sent home for further care at Walter Reed Medical Center. Private Nez risked and sacrificed his life to save his fellow soldier, who only survived due to his bravery and heroism. Formal recommendations for medals and commendations are forthcoming."

Father James processed the information with unfamiliar stoicism. Despite Carlos's best efforts, he was unwilling to dive into his emotions or thoughts right away. He asked for time to process the information, and Carlos departed to join his team at the school.

Patricia Adams arrived on the Navajo Reservation on Monday evening just as the sun began its descent, casting long shadows over the desert landscape. She arrived two days earlier than expected to be with her son. Since hearing the news of Notah's death from Sister Katherine, she had felt a deep, maternal urgency to be by her son's side.

Upon reaching the rectory, she found her only child looking frail and withdrawn, a shadow of the man who had enthusiastically shared his plans for the school and the community just weeks before. His greeting was muted, but he was glad to see her.

After some quiet time just sitting together, Patricia decided to address the trauma directly. While he lay on his bed, Patricia sat at her son's desk and picked up the black picture frame that held a photo of him and Notah taken at graduation. She noted her son's beaming smile and knew how proud he was of the young man he had met only a few months earlier.

"James," she began, her voice soft but firm, "I can't begin to understand the depth of what you're feeling right now. Please talk to me."

Father James's shoulders slumped further as he tried to gather the strength to even discuss his pain.

"Joining the Army was my idea," he said softly. "I led him to believe that was his path, and now he's gone. How could this happen again? First Jess, now Notah. I'm cursed."

Patricia moved to sit beside him, taking his hands in hers.

"James, you gave Notah something precious," she told him. "You gave him hope and a sense of purpose. You helped him see a future for himself that he hadn't imagined before."

He looked into his mother's eyes, searching for a glimmer of absolution that he felt he didn't deserve. Patricia squeezed his hands tighter.

"You saved his life," she said. "I know that may sound impossible to believe right now, but without you, he had no future. You gave him one. Things like this are just out of our control."

She sat next to him and rubbed his head as she'd done countless times before while waiting for him to fall asleep.

In the days that followed, Patricia remained by her son's side. She encouraged him to speak with the grief counselors, to engage with the community that had come to rely on him, and to find solace in the rituals and prayers of his faith. He took her advice, but it didn't make a difference. He felt lonely and jaded. He was just going through the motions.

The day of Notah's funeral arrived under a gorgeous and vast blue sky with less affronting temperatures. The startling beauty of the day seemed incompatible with the somber mood that had enveloped the community. The reservation, usually a place of quiet resilience and natural beauty, was today marked by a palpable sense of loss and mourning. Father James, joined by his mother and hundreds of people from the school, parish, and reservation communities, came to honor their fallen hero whose life had been cut tragically short.

In accordance with a letter Notah had sent to his mother before his deployment to Afghanistan, expressing his wish for a full military funeral should he fall in combat, his service was a departure from Navajo tradition. It was a testament to the profound impact his brief military service had on him, viewing it as a personal journey of growth and an embodiment of the courage and sacrifice for which he wished to be remembered.

The ceremony was performed with deep respect and precise choreography. The folding of the flag, the haunting notes of "Taps" played by a solitary bugler, and the startling sound of the 21-gun salute were all poignant reminders of Notah's service. The flag was then presented to Notah's mother, who accepted it with tears streaming down her face and loved ones by her side.

The community's response to the military honors was a mix of awe and a deep sense of sorrow. For many on the reservation, this was their first experience with a military funeral, and the solemnity and dignity of the proceedings seemed to leave an impression.

With Father James still in a state of shock, he declined the opportunity to address the community at the gravesite. Sister Katherine gave an impromptu eulogy in his place.

"In moments like these, words feel so inadequate, yet they are all we have to offer as we honor the memory of Private

Notah Nez," she began. "Notah was many things to many people—a son, a friend, a classmate, a neighbor. In the last few months, he was also a bright light in our community and a role model for kids across the reservation. He heard and answered a call to serve something greater than himself."

Sister Katherine looked up to collect herself and saw the tears flowing down the face of Father James who stood otherwise stoically in the last row of people gathered to pay their final respects to Notah.

"He put his life in harm's way to protect and defend each of us here today," she continued. "I know many of us have questions. Questions about why this happened, about loss and suffering. I do too. It's natural to seek answers in moments of tragedy. But I believe Notah's life gives us a direction: it shows us the importance of being there for one another, sacrificing for our loved ones, and being a light even when the road feels dark."

She paused again, this time to wipe her own tears from her eyes.

"Notah's journey here has come to an end, but his memory, his love, and his heroism live on in each of us," she said. "Let us be the bearers of his light, sharing it with the world in ways big and small, just as he did. Notah, you will always remain in our hearts. May God welcome you into His kingdom and grant eternal rest upon your soul."

After the funeral, without a word to anyone, Father James got into a car the priests shared to get around the reservation and started driving with no destination in mind. He went west on Route 264 before turning right onto Route 191. His mind was spinning, eyes shedding whatever tears remained, and his right foot pressing forcefully on the gas pedal. In just under an hour, he saw the entrance to Canyon de Chelly National Monument and pulled in. As he walked from his car, the sun began to dip toward the horizon, casting a golden glow over the sprawling tableau surrounding him. The brilliant hues of red, orange, and deep brown of the canyon walls were highlighted by the setting sun's rays.

He walked against the current of tourists who were leaving after a day of experiencing the unmistakable beauty of the canyon and found a path to begin climbing higher for a better view. Finally, he found a spot all to himself to think and escape the too-familiar pain he felt on the reservation. He walked out to the ledge and sat down overlooking the canyon, which, like his guilt, surrounded him.

His eyes traced the intricate layers of rock, and he couldn't help but feel small against such an ancient backdrop. The canyon's shadows grew longer, swallowing the light in the same way darkness seemed to consume his spirit. Just as it had after Jess died, the silence left him isolated with only his tormented thoughts.

In this moment of solitude, Father James grappled with the hopelessness that had driven him to the edge before. He questioned his purpose, his worth as a priest, and the point of his existence if he could not prevent such tragedies. The weight of what could have been, of what should have been, pressed down on him with unbearable force.

As the canyon swallowed the light of day, his thoughts spiraled into a deeper darkness. The silence of the canyon was profound, yet it screamed in his ears—a cacophony of past regrets and missed chances. With each passing moment, the isolation intensified, pressing in on him with an almost physical force.

He looked down almost in a trance, his eyes, void of any more tears, not blinking for some time. Thoughts he'd never felt, even after Jess's death, crept into his mind. He thought about not returning to the reservation and wondered if his absence would truly leave a void or if it would merely be a brief ripple on the surface of the lives he touched.

The last few stragglers trying to exit the canyon before nightfall walked far below him toward the parking lot. He saw a mother and son holding hands and laughing. It broke his focus and made him think of his mom waiting for him back on the reservation. He sat there, alone in the canyon's beauty for a few more minutes. Only the thought of his mom brought him back from the edge and onto the path back to his car.

When he returned to the reservation, he said goodnight to his mom and walked to his room to process the emotional turmoil of the day.

He opened his door and stepped inside. His eyes noticed a small, unfamiliar box at the center of his desk. He saw a note that read, "He'd want you to have this back."

Father James's hands trembled as he picked up the box. He opened it, and his heart felt like it stopped as the box slipped out of his hand. The rosary he'd given Notah before his deployment spilled out of the box and onto his desk.

10

The Letter

Two days after collapsing and injuring his head in the Brigade Chapel, Father James was discharged from the hospital. He was relieved to be heading home, despite the strenuous road ahead. Father Vincent and the parish office manager, Rosemary, picked him up and brought him back to the temporary rectory. Not feeling strong enough to conquer the staircase right away, Father James settled on the living room couch, where he ate his first good meal in days, a hot corned beef sandwich with deli mustard on rye bread from a shop just a few blocks away. After a few days of almost inedible hospital food, Father James enjoyed his lunch on the comfortable couch with a side of his favorite potato chips and a root beer. Despite the terminal diagnosis and unpleasant road ahead, a wave of relief washed over Father James as he felt the familiar comforts of home surround him.

Moments after he wiped the last bit of mustard from his lips, Rosemary opened the front door for Elizabeth, who wanted to check on Father James. She skipped right over the pleasantries and entered the living room with a look of determination.

"Good news," Elizabeth started. "I did some research, and there's a clinical trial at Johns Hopkins that you may qualify for. I called and talked to the trial coordinator and told her all about you. She said to have you come by as soon ...."

"Elizabeth," Father James interjected, taking Elizabeth by surprise. "Thank you, but this isn't how I want to spend my final weeks or months, in a hospital and getting poked and prodded by a team of doctors."

"I know," she said, almost glossing over his concerns. "But it's not so bad. To start, all you have to do is one day of tests—chest X-ray, MRI, bloodwork, and maybe a few other things. I wrote it all down. Then, if you qualify for the trial, you just take pills at home. They call it oral immunotherapy. They only started taking patients this week. They didn't even have this available when you were diagnosed."

"I'm sorry," he said in a dejected tone. "God only knows what those pills will do to me, and I don't want my remaining time spent dealing with the side effects of some trial drug."

"You're right," Elizabeth retorted with a look that showed she wasn't going to give up. "Only God knows. So put your trust in Him. One day of tests. That's it. Then you'll know if you qualify for the drug. Give me one day, please."

He looked down, avoiding eye contact. For the person who saved his life and to whom he had again unburdened himself—this time about the tragic ending to his time on the reservation, he felt he couldn't say no to one day of tests. He looked up and nodded. Elizabeth smiled and ran over to give him a hug, ignoring the trepidation on his face.

Later that week, Elizabeth drove him to Baltimore for his day of testing. The sun was shining brightly on this early spring morning, but Father James was not looking forward to visiting the hospital where he'd been given a terminal diagnosis just months earlier.

As they left town, the state capitol building's dome shrinking in the rearview mirror, Elizabeth turned to Father James briefly before returning her gaze to the road.

"Father, I hope you don't mind, but I'm curious how you ended up here in Maryland after being on the reservation," Elizabeth said with hesitation in her voice.

"Let's see," he said, followed by a long pause. "After Notah, I shut down like I did the year before. I had some good days where I only felt cursed, lost, and alone. I also had bad days where I wondered if there was any point in continuing on."

Father James felt a weight lifted as Elizabeth took the ramp for I-97 North toward Baltimore. It had been two decades, but he'd never really fully opened up to anyone about how he was really feeling.

"After a few weeks, I was an example of the bare minimum level of stability. Essentially, I wasn't going to hurt myself. Otherwise, I was a mess. I decided that the only thing I could do was press on and act like I was fine on the outside. I took a temporary position as a parish priest in Floral Park, New York, a small town on Long Island. They had a priest going through some health concerns, so I helped out for a little more than a year. I kept my distance from activities involving kids and teens, having lost Jess and Notah. I did a lot with senior groups and spent a lot of time visiting parishioners in the hospital. It was hard not only because of the recent tragedies but, as a visiting priest, I never felt like I belonged as a member of the community."

Elizabeth knew it was helpful for Father James to talk, so she just listened and let the conversation go wherever he wanted to take it.

"After New York, I was assigned to the Archdiocese of Baltimore. I spent a few years doing work with Catholic Charities before I was placed at Saint Mary's. I've been at the parish for 16 years now."

For the rest of the car ride, they chatted like old friends, but the conversation halted as Elizabeth entered the Johns Hopkins campus and pulled up to the front of Billings, the main building with a spectacular domed roof. She dropped Father James off while she parked the car. He walked into the lobby and stopped suddenly. Standing directly in the middle of the main entrance, under the dome, was a nearly 11-foot-tall statue of Jesus with his arms out. The white marble statue, as unexpected as it was grand, is known as the "Christus Consolator" and has welcomed visitors to the hospital for more than a century. He'd gone in a different, less inspiring entrance on the sprawling campus a few months earlier when he'd been diagnosed. Maybe this was a sign, he thought. He approached the statue and laid his hands on the feet of Jesus, who stood on a raised platform. He stood, eyes shut, and prayed. Soon, he felt an arm around him. Elizabeth waited until he was ready before they set off for his first appointment.

Once they entered the main corridor just behind the statue, the grandeur and bustling activity of the hospital became immediately palpable. Johns Hopkins had a sterling reputation as a beacon of medical innovation, and it was evident. Father James, although physically weakened by his illness, couldn't help but feel a twinge of hope in this place known for medical breakthroughs, if not miracles.

The testing process was exhaustive and meticulous. Father James was escorted through various departments, each new room bringing a different set of machines and specialists. The chest X-ray was first, where he stood still as the machine hummed and captured images of his lungs. Straight-on-shot, then turn to the right, then turn again. He felt like he was at the local precinct getting his mug shot taken. Next came the MRI scan, with its loud banging sounds and claustrophobic environment. He lay still, trying to calm his racing thoughts while the machine clanged and buzzed around him as the small foam earplugs tried their best to protect his ears. Radiology sent him down the hall to the laboratory where the phlebotomist finally found a vein on her fourth attempt and filled five tubes with his blood. Still not done, it was back to radiology, where he was injected with a tracer before his PET scan.

It was over the top, he thought. But Elizabeth was there with him, keeping a positive attitude, or at least acting like it. Weak from the long day of testing, Elizabeth began pushing Father James in a wheelchair through the hospital's corridors by the end of the day.

"You've certainly earned a treat," she said, sounding like his mom as she helped him back into the wheelchair after the PET scan.

As they left radiology for the final time, Elizabeth pushed Father James down the long corridor they'd spent much of the day traversing. Instead of turning right to head back to the statue of Jesus and the exit, she turned his chair left into the cafeteria and sat him at a table in the back corner of the room, far away from anyone else. The lunch rush was over, and the cafeteria had only a smattering of staff and visitors. Across the room was a doctor with a serious expression on his face as he dug into his sandwich. His white lab coat was hung on the back of his chair, and he was studying the papers he'd spread across the table. Father James caught his eye when the doctor looked up and smiled at the stranger. The doctor, a physician at the Johns Hopkins Children's Center, was still wearing a red foam clown nose, which he certainly used to put his young patients at ease. The doctor, realizing what prompted the smile, removed the nose and gave a big smile back to Father James, who nodded approvingly of the gesture used to help sick kids.

"Here we go," Elizabeth said with a smile and excitement in her voice as she returned to the table with a cheeseburger, fries, and a chocolate milkshake for her companion. "Eat up."

Feeling famished, Father James dug into his burger like he hadn't eaten in a month. There was very little talking at the table as they both focused on their food. The milkshake brought back great memories for Father James. Growing up, he'd make milkshakes with his mom every Saturday when the Gators won a football game. He didn't remember how the tradition started, but he couldn't enjoy a shake without thinking of his mom and the Gators teams of his childhood.

It would soon be three years since Patricia died from congestive heart failure at Shands Hospital in Gainesville. Her son was by her side, holding her hand and praying during her final hours. On the morning she died, her son performed the sacrament of Anointing of the Sick. He knew she couldn't hear or understand what he was saying, but he thanked her for being an incredible, supportive mother.

Moments after he squeezed her hand three times, a sign they'd long used to say, "I love you," she passed away.

"Thank you for being here with me," he said to Elizabeth. "Thank you for never giving up on me."

"Of course," Elizabeth replied warmly, reaching across the table and placing her hand on his. "I wouldn't be anywhere else."

"There's a part of my story I haven't told you," he said, wearing a pained expression on his face. "You saw me on the bridge on Christmas, and you know about the pain I've carried from Jess, Notah, and this diagnosis. But there was another reason I walked to the bridge that night. On top of the pain, guilt, and fear I've felt for years, this was the last straw."

He paused and watched Elizabeth's hopeful expression fade as he fidgeted with his cup and took a sip of his milkshake. His palms were sweaty as the apprehension he felt telling Elizabeth this story took hold of him. His mind churned with the possibilities of her reaction. He worried that the foundation of trust and respect they had built, even over such a short period of time, would waver if he told her, but she deserved the whole truth. Elizabeth had stood by him through thick and thin, her loyalty unwavering, and concealing such a significant part of his current reality felt like a betrayal of the honesty that had always defined their interactions. He needed to trust in the strength of their bond, in her capacity for understanding and compassion.

[180]

"I celebrated Midnight Mass before a standing-room-only congregation at Saint Mary's. It was beautiful — the choir, the Nativity scene on the altar, the poinsettias, the enthusiastic parishioners. It really was one of the best Christmas Masses I've ever been a part of."

He closed his eyes and took another sip. He was searching for courage as the memories came flooding back.

***

Father James walked back up the center aisle at the end of Mass to the sound of the choir singing "O, Come, All Ye Faithful." He shared handshakes, hugs, and Christmas well wishes. The parking lot began to empty out, and he walked back down the aisle toward the altar. One person remained in their seat about halfway down the aisle on the right. The man wore a black hooded sweatshirt, dirty jeans, and well-worn sneakers.

"Merry Christmas," Father James said as the man abruptly stood and turned toward him. His eyes were bloodshot, welled with tears, and appeared manic. "Can I help you, sir?"

Father James didn't recognize the man and began to worry as he found himself alone with a stranger who looked unhinged.

"You don't remember me," the man said incredulously. "Of course you don't. I see you also don't read your mail."

[181]

"My mail?" Father James asked, his expression revealing his confusion.

"I sent you a letter weeks ago to your rectory," the man replied. "I got no response, and I know you wouldn't have forgotten what I wrote."

"I'm sorry, but I'm in a temporary housing situation as the rectory undergoes renovations," Father James replied, still unsure who the man was or what he was talking about. "It must have been lost."

The man's eyes, barely blinking, looked filled with hatred.

"You don't know who I am, but I've never forgotten you," he said, his eyes bulging. "Or my sister."

Father James paused for a moment, and it hit him. He had seen those big blue eyes so many times in his nightmares after the accident. He felt a sudden surge of adrenaline, and his heart began to beat more rapidly.

"Your sister," he said, his voice catching. "Jess."

The man smirked.

"I'm her younger brother, Jason," he said. "Twenty years ago, you not only killed my sister, but you ruined my life. For years, everyone kept saying to forgive you. I couldn't then, and I won't now. That's why I sent you the letter. I wanted you to squirm with dread before your life comes tumbling down, just like mine did two decades ago. The more I think about it, I'm almost glad you didn't get the letter. Now, I get to hand it to you personally. Your life as a priest, it's over."

[182]

He grabbed an envelope from his pocket and slammed it into Father James's chest. Jason bumped his shoulder as he walked toward the church's exit without another word. Father James, stunned and confused, sat in the pew where Jason had waited for him and opened the letter addressed to the Archbishop of the Diocese of Baltimore.

Dear Archbishop,

Father James Adams is a priest at Saint Mary's in Annapolis, but about twenty years ago, he was at my family's parish in New Jersey.

He used to run the youth group at our parish, and my older brother and sister were members of the group. I was still in middle school, but I was often at group activities.

Father James was the cool priest—young and relatable. He was fun to be around. When I was in eighth grade, the group participated in a scavenger hunt. I don't even remember why I was there, but I couldn't participate because I wasn't a group member yet. Father James said I could help him set up the clues. I was very excited to be involved in any way, and I liked being around him.

One of the clues would take students into the woods, so we went there to hide the next clue. While we were in the woods, he put his arm around me.

At first, it didn't bother me. Then, he started to move his hand around to rub my back, which I thought was weird. Then, he

*spun me around, placed his other hand on my genitals, and told
me, "We could have some fun. Nobody needs to know."*

*We were alone in the woods, and I was scared. He assaulted me
and told me that nobody would ever believe me if I told on him
because he's a priest.*

*I'm sorry I never told anyone before, but you should know what
type of priest you have working at one of your churches. Please
make sure he never does this to anyone ever again.*

Sincerely,

Jason Taylor

Father James dropped the letter on the cold, hard ground
below his pew. He sat stunned and expressionless, trying to
absorb the words in Jason's letter. His hands began to
tremble slightly from a surge of emotions that threatened to
overwhelm him. The life he had known, built on decades of
service and compassion was already fragile due to his illness.
Now it was also threatened by a baseless accusation. He
knew the very virtues he had lived by, empathy and
forgiveness, would render him powerless against the tide of
public opinion. Every good thing he'd ever done in his life
would be meaningless after Jason's false accusations became
public. He couldn't live his final months facing abuse
allegations.

As he stood up, a profound fatigue enveloped him, not
just of the body but of the spirit. He walked out of the warm,

festive church to the cold, dark sidewalk. Without a specific plan in mind, he just began walking.

Father James walked through the chilled streets of Annapolis; each step seemed heavier than the last. The festive lights strung across lampposts blurred through the tears he ignored as they fell from his face.

The words of the letter played through his mind. Each time he thought of the accusation, he felt his life's work crumbling. The trust he had fostered, the confidences he had guarded, and the wounds he had helped heal would all be overshadowed by the doubt Jason's words would create. He thought about how people would react to the news. He could see their shock and disappointment and hear their calls to cast him aside.

In a daze, his winding path through Annapolis led him to the foot of the Naval Academy Bridge. He looked up the span to the midpoint of the bridge and saw what seemed like his chance to permanently escape his decades of guilt, the cancer that ravaged his body, and the tarnishing of his reputation.

***

Father James finally found the courage to look up at Elizabeth, who was fidgeting in her seat at the hospital cafeteria table.

As Father James spoke, Elizabeth felt a growing knot of discomfort and worry forming with each word. Her mind

[185]

raced as she listened. She wanted to believe him without a shred of doubt, to dismiss the accusation as the falsehood he declared it to be. As he detailed the impact the accusation had on his life, Elizabeth felt a surge of protectiveness and sympathy. She saw the strain in his eyes and his voice. Yet, her heart ached with the complexity of the situation. She had also only known him for a few months and wasn't fully comfortable outright dismissing the accusation of a potential victim. The tension tugged at her, pulling her thoughts in opposing directions.

"I'm sorry," he said, seeing the discomfort on her face.

An almost uncontrollable coughing fit began. Elizabeth pushed her bottle of water toward him to help but seemed otherwise standoffish.

"I shouldn't have shared that," he said with a raspy voice as the coughing stopped. "I'm tired. We should head back."

Without a word, Elizabeth stood up and began pushing the wheelchair out of the cafeteria and toward the car. Her mind raced the whole way back to Annapolis. The same questions kept crossing her thoughts. Why would he tell me that story if it were true? It can't be true, right? How well do I really know him? Is he sharing this to clear his conscience before he dies?

As she parked the car outside the house on Newman Street, Father James turned to her before leaving.

"Thank you for today," he said. "I pray that you know the accusation is false, but I understand if you need some space."

He opened the car and walked up to the house without assistance as Elizabeth headed back to the Academy.

Father James spent most of the next two days alone in his room, praying and thinking. It had been a few months since Jason gave him the letter, but he'd never heard anything from the diocese or the police. He worried that Elizabeth didn't believe him. She had been such a positive force in his darkest moments, but it had not been long since they were just strangers on the bridge. He was scared to die, especially with this accusation hanging over him.

Father Vincent made sure to bring meals to his colleague's room throughout the day, but it was the only interaction Father James would have until his phone rang. He knew the number. Every call from Johns Hopkins looked as if it was coming from their main phone number.

"Hello, this is James," he answered.

"Father, this is Doctor Francis from the Johns Hopkins clinical trial team," he heard in reply. "I want to thank you for going through all of the tests we put you through the other day. Our team has reviewed the results, and I'm sorry to tell you that you are not a candidate for the trial. In fact, we compared your results to those you had at the time of your diagnosis, and your cancer has advanced significantly. I'm sorry to have to tell you this, but it's time to make plans to enter hospice care."

There was a long pause as Father James absorbed the news. He thought his chances of being accepted into the trial were slim, but he wasn't expecting to hear the doctor recommending hospice. Not yet.

"I understand," he said in a monotone voice. "Thank you for calling."

He hung up the phone and sat motionless, his hands clasped tightly around the phone. The word "hospice" echoed in his mind, a stark reminder of the reality he had been trying to avoid. The familiar feelings of a panic attack surged through his body. He glanced around, seeing the familiar items that had surrounded him in recent months: the worn leather-bound Bible on his bedside table, the faded photograph of his mother smiling warmly, and the rosary she'd given to him that Notah had with him when he died. Each object seemed to hold a piece of his journey that was now taking a definitive turn toward its end.

Father James felt a profound loneliness, a sense of abandonment. Not only was his body abandoning him, but he'd face the end of his life mostly alone. He had dedicated his life to serving others, to being a pillar of faith and support. Now, as he faced his own darkest hour, the absence of a comforting presence was palpable.

He thought about Elizabeth's reaction at the hospital, her sudden distance, and the questions that must have been racing through her mind. He couldn't blame her for her skepticism; the accusation in Jason's letter was damaging and, if believed, would certainly erase the good he had strived to do in his life as a priest. The trust he had built with his parishioners, with Elizabeth, and with the community felt fragile, threatened by the false accusations of a brother who never recovered from his sister's death.

As the evening light faded, casting long shadows across the room, Father James felt deep exhaustion, not just from the physical toll of his illness but from the emotional and spiritual battles he had been fighting. With feelings of abandonment, loneliness, and fear filling his mind, he knew there was only one constant in his life where he could turn.

He sat down on his bed, his body weary, his soul heavy. The future, once a horizon filled with countless possibilities, now seemed narrowed to a path leading to an inevitable end.

Despite the despair that threatened to engulf him, Father James reached for the rosary, its beads worn smooth by the touch of his fingers over the years. He began to pray, not with the fervor of seeking a miracle, but with the quiet resignation of seeking peace. Each "Hail Mary" was a step on a journey of acceptance, each "Our Father" a reminder of the faith that had guided him throughout his life.

11

The Drive

Elizabeth got in her car before dawn, a week after she had taken Father James to Johns Hopkins. She hadn't spoken to him or slept well all week. Over the last few nights, when she couldn't sleep, she had found Jason Taylor on social media and figured out where he lived. With threatening clouds in the sky, she crossed the Bay Bridge from Annapolis to Maryland's Eastern Shore and pointed her car north on Route 301. At this early hour, it would only take about two hours to get to Philadelphia.

Elizabeth had to know the truth. If the accusation was true, she knew it must be reported to both the diocese and the police in New Jersey, where it took place. If Father James had been falsely accused, which she prayed was the case, she knew he would need her desperately. She felt guilty that she had been distant with him, but she had to know.

Feeling like she might fall asleep at the wheel, she stopped at Wawa in Middletown, Delaware. As she got in line to pay for her coffee and breakfast sandwich, she saw a priest, seemingly a regular at the convenience store. He was telling the cashier about how he had just come from the hospital where he was consoling a family who had just lost a loved one. It reinforced how much she hoped to find out that the accusations were just a misguided attempt at revenge by a troubled man. Throughout her life, she had seen the good priests have done in their communities, and she knew every one of Father James's good deeds would be wiped away if the accusations were made public. She got back in her car, feeling more determined than when she left Annapolis.

The final hour of the drive passed in silence, broken only by the steady hum of the engine and the occasional swipe of the windshield wipers. Elizabeth mulled over her questions for Jason, strategizing her approach and pondering her next steps should he be uncooperative.

Elizabeth pulled up to Jason's row house in a struggling neighborhood in North Philadelphia. As she stepped out of the car, her pulse quickened. The neighborhood's worn-down facades and graffiti-splattered walls were a stark contrast to the historic beauty of Annapolis or the idyllic farmland of Vermont she had grown up with. With each step toward Jason's front door, her discomfort swelled—not just from the neighborhood's rough exterior but from the weight of the task ahead. She was about to confront a complete stranger, either about making an incredibly serious false accusation that could ruin a good man's reputation or dig up genuine, deeply rooted pain from his past.

Her stomach churned with an unsettling mix of dread and determination. The idea that she might be confronting someone capable of fabricating such a damning lie was unsettling. If he was lying and felt a hatred for Father James, she feared what else he might be capable of. Yet, a part of her feared the possibility of the accusation being true.

Elizabeth's heart started beating quickly, and her hands trembled slightly as she neared the front door, her mind racing with scenarios. Each thought was punctuated by a stab of guilt for even considering that the accusation might be true. She took a deep breath, trying to steady her nerves and steel herself for the conversation ahead, all the while praying silently that her journey would not uncover a painful truth but would instead vindicate a man she had grown to respect and care for. As she knocked on the door, the questions she had rehearsed a dozen times in the car raced through her mind. She didn't want to be perceived as accusatory or callous. That, she knew, would be the quickest way to a two-hour ride home with no answers after having a door slammed in her face.

Jason opened the door, his unshaven and unkempt face filled with confusion at the stranger who knocked on his door early on a weekend morning. He stood disheveled in the doorway, in loose-fitting gray sweatpants, and a stained white T-shirt.

"Can I help you?" Jason asked, his voice tinged with annoyance toward the unexpected visitor.

"Hi, Jason, my name's Elizabeth," she began, trying to keep her voice steady. "I know you don't know me, but I need to talk to you about something very important to a friend of mine that you know."

She paused as he looked more confused and annoyed that the stranger at his door wouldn't get to the point.

"I don't want to upset you," her preamble continued. "But it's about the letter you wrote about Father James Adams."

Instantly, Jason's demeanor changed. His body language stiffened, and his eyes began shifting around in confusion. Elizabeth felt as if her heart was beating out of her chest. Her rehearsals on the car ride to Philadelphia weren't helping.

"What about it?" he asked, his annoyance turning to frustration. "And who the hell are you?"

He took a half step back from the doorway and shifted his grip on the door as if he was considering abruptly shutting it. Elizabeth gulped and took a deep breath, searching for a way to connect. She didn't want to come all this way just to scare him off immediately.

"I've become close with Father James over the last few months, and he told me about the letter," Elizabeth said. "It really affected him."

"It affected him?" Jason asked sarcastically. "If I'd known it would affect him, I never would have given it to him."

With a look of disgust on his face, and without a word to Elizabeth, he turned his back and started to shut the door.

"I can relate to what you're going through," she shouted with urgency as the door shut with a thud in front of her.

Elizabeth stood in disbelief as the only way to the truth she desperately needed disappeared behind the closed door. Despite the on-and-off drizzle turning into a steadier rain, and without a plan, she took a few steps away from the door and sat down on the steps in front of Jason's rowhouse. She put her head in her hands and replayed her interaction with Jason to identify where she had gone wrong. A few minutes later, she heard the door opening behind her, and she swung her head around to see Jason standing in the doorway. He didn't look any happier than he had a few minutes earlier.

"You need to leave," he said, grabbing the front door to begin shutting it again. "I'm not talking about that man."

"I know about Jess," she replied, hoping to break through to him and start a conversation before he went inside again.

At the mention of Jess, he looked back at Elizabeth and stopped the door from closing again.

"Please," she said, holding her hands up to plead with him for just another moment of his time. "I lost my brother suddenly and unexpectedly just two years ago. I know how it can shatter your world."

Elizabeth's admission caught Jason off guard, and his defensive posture and obvious discomfort with the topic softened slightly.

"My brother shot himself when I was in high school," she said more bluntly than she ever had before. "I haven't and likely never will fully recover. I know how the pain of losing a sibling haunts you."

Jason's initial suspicion wavered as Elizabeth shared her own raw wound—a sibling lost too soon. Her words, earnest and laden with grief that mirrored his own, helped the two strangers find enough common ground to have the difficult discussion Elizabeth needed. His grip on the door loosened, and he walked outside. Without a word, he invited her to sit with him on the front stoop. Elizabeth joined him on the wet, weathered steps and tried to calmly reset the conversation on even ground.

"I'm truly sorry about bringing up your sister like that," Elizabeth said softly, breaking the uncomfortable silence that had settled between them. "It's just... when you lose someone like we have, it feels like you're part of a club you never wanted to join. I didn't know her, of course, but I know the pain."

Jason nodded uncomfortably, his eyes fixed on a crack in the sidewalk.

"Some days are better than others, of course," she admitted. "Talking helps. Not just talking about the pain, but everything. The good memories, good and bad."

"I don't talk about Jess much," he finally said. "It feels like reopening a wound that has barely scabbed over. That pain is what brought me to write that letter. You have no idea what that man did to me. He ruined my life. He took my sister's life. I just need to know that somehow he's going to pay for it."

Elizabeth shifted slightly, feeling the coolness of the concrete underneath her. She looked at Jason, who seemed lost in thought, his gaze distant. She knew she had to tread carefully, yet directly.

"Jason," she began, her voice firm yet empathetic, "I understand your pain, really. But we need to talk about your accusation against Father James. It's very serious and could destroy his life if it's not true."

Jason's eyes flicked back to hers, a flash of anger passing quickly before he masked it with a sigh.

"Look, Elizabeth, you seem nice, but I don't owe you or him anything," he said, his voice tightening. "Nothing happened to him after the accident. He was barely injured, and he just fled town like a coward. No consequences. No justice."

"You're absolutely right," Elizabeth acknowledged. "He caused you incredible pain, and I don't know what he's done to you, but I am here to listen. I just want the truth, not rumors or decades-long anger. Did Father James really do what your letter claims?"

Jason looked away, his jaw clenching.

"Everyone thinks he's this great guy, this living saint because he's a priest and he does stuff in the community," Jason said. "It doesn't erase what happened. It doesn't erase my sister's death."

Elizabeth leaned closer, her once soft voice becoming matter of fact.

"I get it, Jason," she said. "Look, if he did those things you wrote about in the letter, then he's a monster, and to Hell with him. Tell the diocese. Tell the police. Let him face justice."

She took a breath, realizing that he was taken aback by her directness, and softened her approach.

"But," she said with emphasis. "If it's not true, you're ruining an innocent man's life and his legacy."

"Legacy?" he asked, confused at her choice of words.

"He's dying," she told him bluntly. "He has lung cancer. I tried to get him into a clinical trial at Johns Hopkins, but I don't know if he qualified for it. After he told me about the letter you wrote, we haven't spoken. I didn't know what to believe."

Jason's face went blank. News of Father James's terminal illness might have been welcomed news at one point. Today, with Elizabeth sitting just feet away, he just felt pity and guilt. As the barrier between them began to erode, Jason's facade began to crack. His tired blue eyes, filled with years of unshed tears, met Elizabeth's.

"For twenty years, every single day, I've been in pain because of what he did to me," Jason said, the anger bubbling to the surface again. "Jess lit up a room. She was smart, loving, creative. She could have done anything with her life. But, no. Father James gets to keep living after extinguishing her future."

Elizabeth, her own eyes misty, nodded in understanding.

"He didn't do those things to me," Jason said. "I'm just still so angry, so consumed by grief and anger towards him for my sister's death. I wanted him to hurt like I hurt."

He paused for a moment to take a few deep breaths.

"I can't pretend to know all your pain, Jason," she said, relieved to hear the truth. "But lying about Father James won't bring your sister back or give you the peace you're looking for. I can also tell you that there hasn't been a day in the last two decades that Father James hasn't thought about your sister or blamed himself for her death. Endless guilt is his consequence. I'm not asking you to forgive him, but you should know that he's never forgiven himself either."

Jason acknowledged that she was right with a nod.

"I never sent the letter to anyone else," he said, trying to lessen the blow of his actions. "I was never going to. I just wanted him… I just wanted Father James to be looking over his shoulder and scared."

"It worked," Elizabeth replied. "But now he's carrying that fear and worry with him into his final days."

Jason's expression shifted immediately, his face filled with regret.

"I guess I've been carrying this anger and hurt for too long," he admitted, his voice quieter now. "And knowing he's sick... I don't know. It doesn't make things better, but it quiets the anger a bit."

"I hope you can find peace, Jason," she replied as she stood up. "I have a long ride home, and I'm eager to see Father James."

He looked up at her, a semblance of gratitude flickering in his eyes.

"Thank you for coming here today," he said.

She reached out and gave his shoulder a reassuring squeeze. With a final nod, Elizabeth turned and walked down the stoop. With one last wave from the driver's seat, she pulled away and headed out of sight, tears pouring from her eyes and the leftover napkins from Wawa serving a new purpose.

As Elizabeth drove back to Annapolis, the heavy clouds hung low, mirroring the turmoil inside her. Route 301 from Delaware to Maryland was mostly empty, giving her the solitude to delve into the whirlwind of emotions stirred up by her meeting with Jason.

She chastised herself for letting doubt creep in and for not being the anchor Father James needed after confiding in her. The silence she maintained felt like a betrayal, a failure to uphold the unspoken promise of support she had extended to him on the bridge that snowy Christmas morning.

Elizabeth's thoughts were interrupted with memories of their conversations, his gentle demeanor, and the weight of sorrow she had seen in his eyes. In his vulnerability, he had reached out for a lifeline, and she had let it slip through her fingers. She began picturing him alone in his room, grappling with his illness, which was now compounded by the fear of a tarnished legacy that would erase a lifetime of service.

With each passing mile, Elizabeth's resolve strengthened. She felt a deep-seated need to make things right and return to Father James's side, not just as a gesture of solidarity but as an act of penance for her doubt.

The journey back to Annapolis, while physically solitary, was emotionally crowded with Elizabeth's inner dialogue. She spent more than two hours preparing to face Father James again. She felt the need to explain her actions, apologize for her absence, and help carry the burden he would face in his remaining time on Earth.

As Elizabeth crossed the Bay Bridge, just minutes from downtown Annapolis, the familiar sights of the city brought a sense of urgency. She drove straight to the house where Father James was staying, her mind focused only on thoughts of reconciliation and support. Parking hastily, she barely noticed the chill in the air as she rushed to the front door, her heart pounding with a mixture of anxiety and determination.

Father Vincent opened the door, his face smiling to conceal signs of strain and concern for his fellow priest.

"Elizabeth, it's good to see you," he said, stepping aside to let her in. "Come in, I've been hoping you'd come by."

Inside, the atmosphere was calm yet somber as Father Vincent led Elizabeth inside the house where a middle-aged woman was setting up medical equipment and supplies in the corner of the living room.

"This is Amara," Father Vincent said. "She's a home hospice nurse, and she'll be taking care of Father James."

As the word "hospice" hung in the air, a chill passed through Elizabeth, more piercing than the cold she felt on the bridge early on Christmas morning. It was a word she had hoped not to hear, a stark indicator of how grave Father James's situation had become. Clearly, he didn't get into the clinical trial, but she still wasn't expecting hospice already. Her mind raced with thoughts of regret for the time lost, fear of what lay ahead for Father James, and a deep, aching sorrow for the inevitable.

Amara looked up, offering a kind smile to Elizabeth.

"It's nice to meet you," she said, not knowing the relationship between Elizabeth and her new patient. "I'm always happy when my patients have visitors."

Elizabeth nodded, her throat tight with emotion, feeling the weight of the moment.

"Can I see him?" Elizabeth asked as she glanced over toward the staircase, her voice barely above a whisper.

"Of course," Amara replied.

Elizabeth began to climb the stairs to Father James's bedroom, where he insisted he remain. He refused to be on the first floor of the home, dying in front of everyone who walked into the house.

She knocked gently and opened the door.

Elizabeth's heart skipped as she entered the room. Father James was propped up in bed, a shadow of the man she remembered from just a week ago. The speed at which the cancer was ravaging him startled her. His eyes, once full of life and warmth, were tired but lit up when they met hers.

"Elizabeth," Father James breathed out, his voice weak but filled with happiness and relief. "You came back."

Tears formed in Elizabeth's eyes as she approached the bedside, grasping his hand gently.

"I'm so sorry I haven't been here," she choked out, the guilt and regret pouring from her in a flood of emotion. "I should have believed in you."

Father James gave a weak but forgiving smile, squeezing her hand with the little strength he had left.

"You're here now, that's all that matters," he whispered, the kindness in his eyes easing some of her pain. "I don't have much time, which I'm sure you put together. It's a great comfort to have you here with me."

Elizabeth sat by his side, recounting her journey to Philadelphia, her meeting with Jason, and the revelation of the truth behind his false accusations. Father James listened quietly, nodding slightly, his face a mixture of sadness and forgiveness.

"Jason is still in pain," Elizabeth said, her voice steadying as she spoke. "He admitted that the accusations were false, driven by his unresolved grief and anger."

Father James closed his eyes for a moment, a tear escaping down his cheek.

"Thank you for seeking the truth, Elizabeth," he said. "Of course, I knew it was a lie, and I actually did feel bad because I knew it came from a place of pain. But I've been living in fear that I would forever be remembered for that lie. You've brought me peace. Thank you."

The room was filled with silence, as Elizabeth continued to hold Father James's hand, her presence a comforting balm to his weary soul. At that moment, the weight of her guilt began to lift, replaced by a solemn commitment to stay by his side, to support him through his final journey.

12

The Visitors

It didn't take long for word to get out about Father James's deteriorating condition. Friends, parishioners, and colleagues from throughout his life came to visit and spend a final few moments with him. Father Vincent and Elizabeth, when she had any free time from her busy and structured life as a Midshipman, served as greeters and hosts. There were more casseroles and baked ziti than could fit in the fridge, but there were also always enough guests to eat the food. The comments on Saint Mary's Facebook page were filled with prayers, well-wishes, and fond memories of time spent with their priest. Twice a day, Rosemary would print the messages at the nearby parish office and walk them over to read to her ailing colleague. She could tell how much the messages meant to him.

The outpouring of love and support was seen at each Mass on Sunday. Father Vincent felt that Mass attendance spiked

[204]

as people came together to prepare for the death of a critical member of their parish community. Saint Mary's even saw a burst of generosity from their congregation in their weekly collection. After the last Mass that Sunday, the choir walked down Newman Street to sing some of Father James's favorite hymns from the sidewalk below his bedroom window. People just walking around Annapolis who stopped to listen to the music were moved by the touching tribute.

The next evening, the prayer group from the Naval Academy took the short walk from The Yard to pray with their group's leader. Emily even brought a fresh batch of the peanut butter blossoms that she'd made for Father James shortly after Christmas. She reminded him of the scripture they'd read together that night from the Book of Philippians. It stuck with her, she said, as she contemplated her future in the Navy and thought it applied to his future beyond his life on Earth.

Forgetting those things which are behind, and reaching forth unto those things which are before.

"Although your time on Earth may be ending, eternal life with Christ is still before you," she said.

His voice, very raspy from the coughing fits, wasn't up to speaking. He squeezed her hand and gave a nod of thanks.

Each knock at the door heralded another visitor, another person to greet with a smile that demanded more of him than anyone could know. He felt profound gratitude for each face that appeared, familiar ones steeped in shared histories and newer ones marked by recent bonds of spiritual kinship. Yet, with each warm embrace, each handshake, his heart ached with a bittersweet pang.

His mind trembled slightly under the weight of his impending farewell. He was touched deeply by the love and support, but each well-wisher also reminded him of the inevitable—the approaching end of his life on Earth. Though he managed to keep his composure, offering words of comfort and even sharing laughter when his body allowed, inside, Father James felt the loneliness that only comes with the finality of goodbye. It was as if with each farewell, a small piece of him was already drifting away, loosening his ties to this world and preparing him for the next.

On Tuesday, Father Vincent brought a stack of letters and cards upstairs. He was grateful for the break in the stream of visitors. It gave him the chance to spend a few minutes with his friend. He grabbed an envelope with an Arizona return address. He unfolded the letter and read it aloud.

Dear James,
I'm sorry that we lost touch over the years. Please know
that you have remained a constant in my prayers.
Your time living in our community was short. Still, your
impact lives on.
For years now, students at Saint Michael's have
participated in the FaithWorks program you developed
but never had the opportunity to see brought to life.

Now, hanging at the main school entrance is a sign with the words you preached and lived.

"Show me your faith without your works, and I will show you my faith by my works."

You have been, and continue to be, a force for good in the world.

Since I heard about your health, the entire Saint Michael's community has been praying for you each day before school. I'm excited to tell you that Etta Hoskie, a member of this year's graduating class, will be the first person awarded the annual Father James Adams Award for showing their faith through service to the community.

I am forever grateful for our short, but meaningful time together.

Sending you love and prayers from the Saint Michael's community and the entire Navajo Nation.

Yours in Christ,

Katherine

As Father Vincent's voice filled the quiet room, reading each word from Sister Katherine's letter, Father James felt a warmth spread through him, contrasting sharply with the coolness of his weakening body. Father Vincent held up the photographs enclosed in the letter, including several of a young Father James and Notah. His eyes, though tired, sparkled momentarily as he was transported back to the vibrant landscapes and resilient spirits of the Navajo Nation.

A photo they took at the baseball game, which Father James had never seen before brought back wonderful memories. Each word resonated deeply, not just as a reminder of the impact he had during his brief tenure there but as a testament to the enduring bonds he had forged. Hearing that his FaithWorks program still launched after his departure and continues today brought great comfort.

Father Vincent, wiping away tears as he finished the letter, looked down at his friend. Father James didn't say a word, but his face beamed with pride and joy. His brief time on the reservation ended in tragedy, but his love for the community always remained with him. Noticing Father James's uneven breaths and seeing the emotional toll of the letter, Father Vincent put the letters down and stood up.

"Get some sleep, James," he said, pulling the blanket over his friend.

"Thank you, Vincent," he replied. "For everything."

Father Vincent forced a smile under the circumstances and turned off the bedroom lights as he left.

After a few hours of rest, Rosemary came to bring Father James dinner and to read the latest messages sent on social media. She sat at his bedside and helped Father James eat while reading well-wishes.

"You got a long one today," Rosemary said with a smile, pulling it out of the large stack of notes.

Dear Father James,

I'm not sure if you'll remember me, but I was in your youth group twenty years ago. We haven't spoken since the accident after the dance.

I saw on Facebook that you were ill, and I wanted to write because it's been so long. After such a long time, I have a different and more mature perspective than I did as a kid in high school.

I know, and everyone knows, that what happened with Jess was an accident. There is no blame. There was some back in 2003, but we were young and grieving.

I'm now 37 and a mom of twin seven-year-old girls—Jessica and Taylor.

They are my way of keeping her memory alive.

Please know that you are in my prayers each day, and the entire parish has been praying for you at Mass since we heard about your diagnosis.

It's been a long time, but the good you did here was never forgotten.

With gratitude,

Lauren Rodriguez

Father James mustered a smile and a few tears. Of course, he remembered Lauren. She was basically attached at the hip with Jess and their friend Maggie. He smiled thinking about her as a mom with twins and was so touched by their names, Lauren's tribute to her late friend.

There was a soft knock at the door before Father Vincent walked slowly into the bedroom.

"Rosemary, would you give us the room?" he asked.

The parish office manager gathered her papers and set them down on the bedside table before heading downstairs. Father Vincent sat down in the recently vacated seat, his face etched with discomfort.

"Jim, you have a visitor downstairs asking to see you," he said cautiously. "I didn't know what to do, so please let me know if you want me to ask him to leave. He says that he's Walter Adams, your father."

A surge of emotions came over Father James, and his face showed his disbelief. As he processed the shock, his mind raced through a mix of feelings. He felt bitter, a reignited feeling of abandonment, and strong, unresolved anger. Yet, underneath these turbulent sensations, there was a flicker of curiosity, a quiet wonder about why his father would choose to come now after all these years. His father, if he was still alive, would be 80 years old, and he hadn't seen or heard from him in more than three decades. After a brief coughing fit, he gathered his thoughts.

"I'm not sure I believe it," he told Father Vincent. "But, you can send him upstairs. If nothing else, this should be interesting."

Father James heard only the murmurs of conversation downstairs, followed by the slow, methodical sound of footsteps nearing. The door, left slightly ajar, squeaked as it slowly opened. The man who stood in the doorway was both a stranger and a ghost from a life long abandoned. An elderly man stood like a statue in the doorway, holding a small bag in his right hand. He was a shell of the man Father James knew as a child, but it was undoubtedly his father. Although considerably aged, his face was that of the man he'd once hated, feared, and held at gunpoint to force him out of his own home. His hair, now grayed and thinned, was still combed and styled like the man he knew in the 1980s. His eyes, tired and calm, didn't match the menacing look he was used to from a lifetime ago.

Father James's heart quickly hammered against his ribs. A complex storm of anger, abandonment, and an unexpected twinge of empathy overwhelmed him. His mind flashed back to the living room of their Florida home, and he could still hear the shotgun firing into the chair and the smell that lingered. His father's departure left a void filled with years of unanswered questions and unresolved anger. Here too, he thought, was the last chance to heal the long-ago scabbed-over wound. Father James's eyes locked onto the figure standing in the doorway. The silence between them was heavy, filled with the weight of decades of absence and unspoken words.

"Oh, Jimmy," he finally said, barely louder than a whisper. "I don't know what to say. I just knew I had to come here and see you."

Walter grabbed the door frame for support and began trying to control his breathing. The emotions of seeing the son he abandoned overwhelmed him, but seeing him at the end of a battle with lung cancer was too much to bear.

Father James shifted in his bed, his eyes never leaving the man who had been absent for the majority of his life but now stood before him. The room was thick with tension, each second stretching longer than the last.

"Three decades," Father James began, his voice low and steady. "More than three decades, and not a single word. Why now, after all this time?"

"I heard about your health," Walter replied, looking down and feeling filled with shame.

He walked completely into the room and sat at his son's bedside.

"It shook me, knowing there wasn't much time," he continued. "I'm so sorry."

"Sorry?" Father James echoed, bitterness lacing his tone. "Do you even know what leaving did to us?"

"I can't begin to understand the pain I caused, and I'm not here to make excuses," his father replied, his eyes pleading for some semblance of understanding. "I was… I am selfish and weak."

For a moment, the tension in the room quietly hung thick around them. Neither of them knew what to say.

"You may not believe this, but I've been following your work at this parish for a few years," Walter shared, breaking the uncomfortable silence. "I watch every one of your Masses that the church livestreams on the internet from home in Texas. A neighbor's granddaughter showed me how to set it up on my phone. So, there I am, alone on my couch but comforted by your presence every Sunday."

Father James looked away, his gaze settling on the small crucifix hanging on the wall to collect his thoughts.

"You missed so much," he said. "Graduations, my ordination, the life I built without you, mom's illness."

The room felt smaller as the past pressed in, a lifetime of missed moments and silent questions hanging between them. Father James felt the bed shift beneath him as he struggled to sit up a bit more, driven by a need to face his father not just as a son, but as a man who had lived a full life in his absence.

"I'm a coward, son," Walter said with confidence. "That day you pointed the shotgun at me, you were stronger in that moment than I've been in my whole life. I've always been a quitter, and I thought that you wouldn't want to see me after such a long time. At least that's what I told myself to ensure that I'd never have to face you. Then, I heard about your cancer, and I couldn't stay away any longer. I'm sorry— for everything."

They sat in silence, the years of separation and the pain it caused stretching out between them. Father James felt his emotions churning inside him, but the anger that had once burned so fiercely had dimmed. He didn't know if he just didn't have the energy to be mad or if it was his changed perspective on life, but it wasn't anger that he felt looking at his father. Now, on his deathbed, he was overcome with sadness for what could have been and a strong desire for closure.

"I know that I'm the last person in the world who should be asking you for a favor, but that's exactly what I'm going to do," Walter said.

He slowly bent down and picked up the bag he had brought into the room. He reached inside and removed his son's stole, the fabric he wore around the neck when celebrating Mass or performing sacraments.

"I asked the priest downstairs about what I'd like you to do for me," Walter said hesitantly. "He said you'd need this."

Seeing the stole, Father James felt a flutter in his chest. Without a word, Walter managed to wrap the stole behind his son's neck and drape it over his chest. Then, he backed up his chair and slowly kneeled on the ground beside his son's death bed.

"Forgive me, Father, for I have sinned," he started. "It has been 73 years since my last confession."

Stunned at the sight of his father on his knees asking for forgiveness, Father James quickly shifted away from his role of sad, abandoned son to that of a priest tending to his flock. He nodded for his father to continue. The weight of the sacramental stole draped over his shoulders suddenly felt more substantial, grounding him in his vocation in a way he hadn't felt much since entering hospice care. This wasn't just a personal reconciliation; Father James's role as a priest was being called into service one more time in one of the most intimate, painful ways imaginable.

"There are too many sins to list or even remember, but the biggest sin is my failure as a father and husband. I was a complete failure at the two most important jobs I ever had. There is no excuse for how I treated my wife and son."

He paused, and his head fell onto the mattress, which was at eye level. The sheets absorbed his tears and muffled his cries. He looked up at his son and composed himself enough to continue.

"I wasn't there for you or your mom before I left. I hit your mother, drank too much, and made your lives miserable. Then, I was a coward and left you. You were right to point that gun at me. You stood up for yourself and your mother. The only good thing I did in my wasted life was have a son who devoted his life to more than balancing out the stain on this world that I've been. I'm sorry for these and all my sins."

"Praying will help you," Father James responded. "But you can't just say five Hail Marys and Our Fathers and move on. Your penance is to find a way to be a force for good in your remaining years, even when I'm gone."

His father bowed his head to recite the Act of Contrition.

Celebrating the sacrament offered an opportunity for father and son to begin a conversation. They eased into it but ended up spending more than an hour reminiscing about the few good memories they shared together and talked about one of their only shared loves — the Florida Gators.

"You need to rest, son," his father said during a lull in the conversation, noticing Father James's fading energy. "I'd like to come back in the morning if you'll have me."

Father James agreed and watched his father leave, the door closing softly behind him. In the silence that followed, he felt an unexpected sense of closure. The end of a chapter of his life that had always been open and raw was finally, if not fully healed, at least acknowledged and understood.

After a surprisingly restful night, the soft morning light crept through the curtains of Father James's room, casting a gentle glow. His sleep had been deep and undisturbed, a rare gift given his recent restless nights. Despite having very little appetite lately, he ate a hearty breakfast with his father. Their conversation went in many directions, but it was positive. They didn't dwell on their painful shared past. Instead, they reconnected as much as they could under the circumstances. Father James was thankful for the time they had together, even after such a long absence.

Not long after Walter left, more visitors began coming and going. Amara gave him his medicine and told him another visitor was waiting. Thinking it was another parishioner, he was shocked to see Jason Taylor hesitantly step into the bedroom, his posture reflecting a mixture of regret and resolve. His heart, already heavy with the weight of his illness and the shocking visit from his father, now beat with a blend of apprehension and hope. There stood a figure so closely tied to a past tragedy, one that haunted both their lives, and a man who threatened to destroy him on Christmas morning.

"Father James, I... I came to apologize," Jason stammered, his voice thick and his eyes heavy with years of unshed tears.

He took a step inside, his eyes not quite meeting Father James's.

"I've been living with this anger and pain for more than twenty years," he continued. "I was wrong to take it out on you."

Father James, who had to ration his voice to prevent coughing attacks, motioned for Jason to sit next to him. Jason hesitated before taking the seat, the weight of his guilt almost visible on his shoulders.

"I've dealt with addiction and alcoholism for years," he admitted with a look of shame. "I fell off the wagon again a few months ago. That's when the anger and eagerness for revenge returned. Your friend, the young lady from the Naval Academy, found me recently. She just showed up at my house in Philadelphia, which was odd at first, but she'll never fully know how much her visit meant to me. Facing her and hearing her story helped me find the closure I've sought for two decades. I haven't used or had a drink since she left, and God willing, I never will again."

"I'm sorry to hear what you've been through," Father James whispered, moving his head as close to Jason as possible. "Please know there hasn't been a day that I haven't thought about Jess. I can never undo the pain caused by that accident, and I am so sorry for the loss and suffering it brought to you and your family."

Jason nodded, the barriers of anger and resentment that had fortified his heart for so long beginning to crumble.

"Talking to you now and talking to Elizabeth, I know of the burden you've carried all these years," he said. "I forgive you. I should have been able to say that decades ago, but I couldn't. I held onto the pain, the anger, and the blame. I hated you for so long, but I shouldn't have. Please forgive me."

Father James smiled and placed his hand on Jason's arm.

"All is forgiven," he said. "But I need you to do something. Get the help you need, and stay clean. Do it for Jess."

Jason nodded in agreement.

"I will," he agreed. "For Jess."

Father Vincent walked in with lunch. Despite the short visit, Jason knew it was time to leave, having accomplished his goal. They said goodbye and wished each other well. Father James felt a profound sense of relief as the long-held pain between them had been acknowledged and addressed, allowing a glimmer of hope and healing to emerge from decades of sorrow and regret. The visit, brief as it was, marked a significant step toward closure for both men, a balm to their long-tormented souls.

As Jason left, Father James leaned back against his pillows, a sense of peace washing over him. For the first time in twenty years, he felt completely forgiven for the accident. Now, he was ready to forgive himself.

He closed his eyes and felt like the weight he'd carried every day of his life since 2003 had been taken off his shoulders. He reflected on the journey that had brought him to this moment. He thought of Jess, her vibrant spirit, and the light she had brought into the lives of those who knew her. Those thoughts, once an unbearable source of pain, now brought him comfort. He was glad to face whatever time he had left with a heart unburdened by guilt and a soul at peace with the past.

As the day waned into evening, he enjoyed the peaceful quiet, save for the occasional murmur from downstairs. Now, he enjoyed a feeling of weightlessness, his pain and emotional trauma replaced by forgiveness and peace. He smiled, thinking about the letters from Sister Katherine, Lauren, and dozens of parishioners past and present.

Amidst these reflections, Father James felt the immense power of forgiveness and the indelible mark of genuine human connection. He thought about all the times he'd offered the sacrament of reconciliation without personally feeling its power. The grievances with his father and the threats from Jason had dissolved, leaving behind a clarity and understanding that life, in all its complexity, was inherently valuable and worthy of redemption.

Elizabeth, back after another long day at the Academy, quietly entered the room. Her presence was a comforting reminder of the new relationships he had formed in his final months. Their shared experiences, the vulnerabilities they exposed to each other, had forged a bond that was both unexpected and deeply cherished. She sat in the chair next to him and put his hand in hers.

"Father," Elizabeth whispered, "how are you feeling?"

Father James turned to her and smiled more genuinely than at any point since she first met him.

"Honestly, I'm good," he said with confidence. "Thank you for the gift of these last few months. Without you, there would have been no closure."

He paused, looked at her, and squeezed her hand.

"I'm ready."

13

The Anointing

Father Vincent turned off the lights in the bedroom. The room was now intimately lit by candlelight. He walked slowly and quietly to the bedside where Father James lay. Father Vincent was used to performing this part of his priestly duty on strangers or parishioners, not close friends or colleagues. Having known Father James for more than a decade, celebrating this sacrament with him was quite emotional. Though he was devastated to be losing someone close to him, he felt honored to be able to give Father James this gift.

"Are you ready, Jim?" he asked.

Father James, his eyes locked on his friend, nodded. He was perfectly still and focused on the spiritual significance of the sacrament he was about to receive. He reflected on the many times he had stood by bedsides, offering comfort and spiritual solace to those at the brink of their earthly existence.

He remembered their faces, their silent thank-yous, their tear-filled eyes.

Father James felt a deep connection to his own mortality and the journey of his faith, both as a shepherd to his flock and now as a sheep amongst it. The sacrament, which had always been a conduit of God's grace and healing to others, was now a personal encounter with the divine for him. There was a bittersweet recognition of his vulnerability and a relinquishing of his pastoral role in the most personal way possible.

Each movement by Father Vincent, even a tiny adjustment to his vestments, echoed with profound intimacy in the dimly lit room, illuminated only by the gentle flicker of candlelight. Despite the thoughts and emotions bouncing around his head, Father James also felt at peace as he embraced this sacred moment—a final anointing not just of the body, but of his life. Father Vincent stood over him and began.

Lord God, you have said to us through your apostle James: "Are there people sick among you? Let them send for the priests of the Church, and let the priests pray over them, anointing them with oil in the name of the Lord. The prayer of faith will save the sick persons, and the Lord will raise them up. If they have committed any sins, their sins will be forgiven."

Lord, we have gathered here in your name and we ask you to be among us, to watch over our brother James. We ask this with confidence, for you live and reign forever and ever.

"Amen," Father James said as loud as he could manage.

Father Vincent, standing over the bed, laid his hands on his friend's head and prayed silently. For a moment, he was more than a priest performing a sacrament. He was also a man offering comfort and affection to a dying friend, a role with which Father James was very familiar. Father Vincent, meticulous in every motion, bent down and retrieved the oil used in the sacrament. Dipping his thumb in the sacred oil, he made the sign of the cross on Father James's forehead.

Through this holy anointing may the Lord in his love and mercy help you with the grace of the Holy Spirit.

"Amen," Father James repeated.

As he'd done on the forehead, Father Vincent took the oil and anointed Father James's hands.

May the Lord who frees you from sin save you and raise you up.

"Amen," Father James said once more.

With Father James's hands in his own, he began to pray as his friend, who didn't have the energy to recite the Lord's prayer aloud, joined in by mouthing the words.

"Amen," they said together at the prayer's conclusion.

Father Vincent took a moment and let the silence and solemnity of the moment breathe before continuing with a post-anointing prayer.

Lord Jesus Christ, you chose to share our human nature, to redeem all people, and to heal the sick. Look with compassion upon your servant James, whom we have anointed in your name with this holy oil for the healing of his body and spirit. Support him with your power, comfort him with your protection, and give him the strength to fight against evil. Since you have given him a share in your own passion, help him to find hope in suffering, for you are Lord forever and ever. May the blessing of almighty God, the Father, and the Son, and the Holy Spirit, come upon you and remain with you forever.

"Amen," Father James said one last time.

Father James felt a poignant connection to every soul he had comforted at the end of their life. Now, having received the sacrament himself, his thoughts were no longer focused on his own mortality. Instead, he was overwhelmed by an incredible sense of peace. The pain of his father abandoning him and his mother, losing Jess in the accident, and Notah's sacrifice was suddenly lifted from his shoulders. He was comforted by a deep gratitude for the full life he had been granted. The weight of his earthly duties seemed to melt away and was replaced by an inner serenity, knowing that he had served well and was now entrusting himself to his eternal reward. Father Vincent sat down next to the bed and prayed in silence as his friend fell asleep. Before leaving the room, he placed Father James's rosary, which had fallen onto the side of his bed, in his hands.

***

After waking from a nap a few hours later, Father James lay in bed. He looked around his bedroom and felt a strange sensation. He felt clear-headed, alert, and filled with a burst of energy. He didn't feel like a man on his deathbed, and he didn't want to look like one either. He was at his wit's end with lying in bed all day just waiting to die. He devoted his life to his vocation, and he wanted to spend his remaining time with the dignity of feeling and looking like a priest.

Not wanting anyone to help him, Father James used every ounce of energy he had to get out of his bed. He gingerly walked across his room to the closet. Hanging in his closet was a freshly pressed, long unused black shirt and matching slacks. Slowly, he got dressed as if he was going to celebrate Mass like he'd done hundreds of times before. After catching his breath, he slid his socks over his feet and tied his shoes tightly. Finally, he adjusted the white clerical collar properly underneath his crisp shirt.

He looked back into his closet and noticed a black jacket. He slowly took it off its hanger and unzipped it. Instead of sending his emotions into a tailspin thinking about the night Elizabeth draped it over his shivering body, he placed the jacket against his face and smiled. He thought about how lucky he was on the bridge. Without Elizabeth, he would not have found peace.

Still smiling and holding the jacket, Father James looked in the mirror. His clothes were loose on his body, which had abandoned him, but he was proud that he was able to accomplish this once simple task. He felt good seeing a priest in the mirror rather than a man on his deathbed. For a moment, he wasn't just a patient confined to the suffocating bounds of his illness. He was a servant of God, a shepherd of his flock. The reflection staring back at him brought a fleeting but meaningful sense of purpose and normalcy.

His thoughts drifted to the many times he had stood before this same mirror, adjusting his collar, preparing to lead his congregation in prayer. The sense of anticipation, the feeling of readiness, all came flooding back. Today, in this small act of donning his clerical clothes, he reclaimed a part of himself he thought was lost to the relentless progression of his disease.

Memories of his first days in the seminary surfaced—days filled with youthful optimism and a burning desire to serve. The image in the mirror transported him back to those early mornings, the smell of incense and the sound of hymns echoing through the chapel. The contrast between then and now was stark, yet at this moment, he felt a bridge between the past and the present. His identity as a priest had been a constant, his anchor, and seeing that reflected back at him was an important reminder that, despite everything, his essence remained untouched.

The fleeting burst of energy might soon wane, and the clarity might fade, but for now, he cherished the moment.

***

Just about three-quarters of a mile away, Elizabeth began climbing on top of her fellow classmates. They boosted her higher and higher. She was sweating, and her hands were covered in grease, but her fellow Naval Academy plebes cheered her on. For more than two hours, her classmates had formed a base of tall Midshipmen with incredibly strong legs. Now, there were three levels of Midshipmen standing on each other's shoulders, desperately trying to climb the 21 feet necessary to scale the greased-up Herndon Monument.

The tradition, which dated back more than 60 years, marked the end of the first year at the Academy and forced the young men and women to work together to replace the plebe-style Midshipmen hat, often called the "dixie cup hat" with an upperclassman hat. Plebe year only ends after the class scales the monument and replaces the hat.

She started to get some momentum as a few classmates held her ankles and thighs steady to offer more support. Tall, athletic, but light, Elizabeth was the perfect candidate to climb to the top of the monument.

"Just a little higher!" she yelled to nobody in particular, looking down at the mass of humanity below her.

Her classmates passed up towel after towel to her so she could wipe away some of the 300 pounds of vegetable shortening that covered the monument. She'd wipe away a section, throw the towel down, and start again. Soon, she was making progress up the monument and feeling like she may actually make it.

Each level of Midshipmen, most of them shirtless and pouring sweat, gave everything they had to give Elizabeth one last boost. Her right hand stretched as far as it could. She grabbed the brim between her index and middle finger and tried to pull herself up just another inch or two. With one last, unexpected boost from below, she grabbed the hat and pulled it off the top of the point of the Washington Monument-style structure. The crowd erupted below, and she slid down over her friends and classmates just as the human pyramid began to collapse. Everyone started jumping around her to celebrate.

Plebe year was over.

As Elizabeth clung tightly to the hat, her descent from the greased monument was a flurry of emotions. The thrill of being the one to reach the top pulsed through her veins. Her classmates' cheers washed over her like a victorious wave, filling her with a deep sense of accomplishment and pride. Yet, as she landed back on the ground, supported by the sea of hands that had boosted her to success, her thoughts were divided. Part of her reveled in the completion of this storied tradition. However, amid the exuberance, a part of her mind was across town, in the room where Father James lay in a starkly different setting. As her classmates headed out for a celebration, Elizabeth went back to the barracks to shower and change. She was eager to share the news that she was the one who finished the Herndon Monument Climb with Father James.

After a jog from the Academy, Elizabeth was greeted by Rosemary with a warm hug.

"He's doing well today," she said before the obvious questions could be asked. "More energy, and he's certainly in better spirits. Father Vincent gave him the sacrament this morning, the Anointing of the Sick. Who knows? Maybe that helped. Father Vincent and I were stunned by his unexpected turnaround, but Amara said she's seen this before with patients shortly before the end."

Before she could reply, Rosemary was off to tend to something in the kitchen where Father Vincent was preparing food. It had a delicious and familiar smell that made Elizabeth think about her childhood. She walked into the kitchen and saw Father Vincent removing a perfectly browned grilled cheese with melted cheese oozing out from one side of the skillet, the leftover butter still bubbling. Rosemary poured hot tomato soup into a bowl and sprinkled some of the remaining cheese on top.

"It's his favorite meal," Father Vincent said with a chuckle. "So simple, but he really loves it."

"It smells incredible!" Elizabeth said, hungry from the exhausting afternoon. "I was about to go up. I can take the food with me."

Elizabeth meticulously assembled the wooden tray to ensure she wouldn't spill the hot soup or the tall glass of water on her way up the stairs. She walked from the kitchen through the living room and to the foot of the stairs, where she adjusted her grip. For a few moments, the only sound in the house was that of her feet slowly and carefully walking up the staircase one slow step at a time. As she arrived at the top of the stairs and turned toward Father James's bedroom, she was relieved to see the bedroom door slightly ajar.

"You're not going to believe..." Elizabeth said, her voice stopping abruptly.

Downstairs, the only sound they heard was the crashing of the tray and the dishes hitting the floor, some of it now flying down the staircase.

In that breathless instant, as Elizabeth's eyes fell upon Father James, a torrent of thoughts overwhelmed her. The sudden sight of him, vulnerable and motionless, triggered a visceral flashback to the darkest day of her life just two years earlier. Panic gripped her heart and left a stunned, open-mouthed expression on her face.

The moments after the dishes crashed to the floor were eerily silent until the house was filled with Elizabeth's urgent plea.

"Hurry!" she yelled. "Father Vincent! Rosemary!"

As they hurried toward the staircase, Elizabeth ran into the bedroom, where she found Father James lying face down and diagonally across his bed on top of his blanket. She ran to him and turned him over.

"Father!" she shouted, having flashbacks to finding her brother in the barn. "Father James, can you hear me?"

Father Vincent and Rosemary navigated the spilled food and broken dishes to make their way into the room to find Elizabeth crying, her head pressed down on her friend's motionless chest. Father Vincent came over and calmly placed two fingers on his friend's neck to check for a pulse. Without a word, he helped Elizabeth up. Then, he moved Father James fully onto his back and comfortably on the bed.

Elizabeth, still processing the scene in front of her, was surprised to see Father James wearing his priest attire. Then, she saw his most prized possession, the rosary from his mother, on the floor next to the bed. She picked it up, held it tightly, and closed her eyes. She stood at the bedside, leaned down, and placed the rosary in Father James's hands. Father Vincent held Elizabeth's hand on one side and Rosemary's hand on the other side as he began to pray.

Saints of God, come to his aid!
Come to meet him, Angels of the Lord!
Receive his soul and present him to God the Most High.
May Christ, who called you, take you to himself;
May Angels lead you to Abraham's side.
Give him eternal rest, O Lord,
and may your light shine on him forever.

Elizabeth barely heard the prayer, her gaze and thoughts wholly focused on Father James's hands. Seeing the rosary that meant so much to him safely back in his grasp brought her comfort even as her tears traced paths down her cheeks. The weight of grief was heavy on her shoulders, yet there was an undercurrent of relief and gratitude. She was relieved that Father James no longer had to endure the physical suffering that had so visibly drained him. She was filled with gratitude for the moments of reconciliation and redemption he experienced in his final days. His reunion with his estranged father and the heartfelt confession that followed closed a long and painful chapter in his life. Jason's visit and their mutual forgiveness allowed Father James to conclude his life's story on his own terms, with a sense of completeness and serenity. The letters, messages, and outpourings from people he knew throughout his life brought happiness and a sense of his duty on Earth being complete.

Elizabeth's mind replayed their discussions about life, faith, and purpose. She thought about how Father James faced his impending end with a blend of realism and hope, how he embraced his fate not with resignation but with an acceptance that sought to bring peace to those he was leaving behind. His life, though ending, left ripples of influence that extended far beyond the confines of his room.

In the quiet of the room, with only the soft whispers of the others' prayers filling the space, Elizabeth felt a profound connection to the man who had become not just a spiritual guide but a cherished friend. The pain of loss was sharp, yet in it, she found a deep sense of privilege for having known Father James and for being part of his final journey.

As Father Vincent and Rosemary left the room to call the funeral home, Elizabeth lingered a moment longer, her gaze

fixed on Father James. Her eyes traced the familiar lines of
his face, now still. Elizabeth reflected on how Father James
had faced his mortality with dignity and courage, and she
whispered a personal goodbye— a silent promise to carry
forward the lessons learned and the love shared.

14

The Monument

Elizabeth, alone in the barracks, made the final adjustments to her uniform. She put on her white coat, with its six gold buttons, and placed her new upperclassman hat on top of her blonde hair styled with a bun. She looked in the mirror and saw a face filled with nervous anticipation staring back.

On this morning, she would stand before a packed church to honor Father James's life in front of his family, friends, and parishioners—a task she felt deeply honored yet daunted to perform. Elizabeth initially declined the opportunity to speak because she felt she hadn't known him long enough. There had to be more qualified people, she insisted. It wasn't until Father Vincent let her know that it was a request Father James made earlier in the week that she agreed.

Her thoughts were filled with memories and sentiments about the man who had become not just a mentor but a friend over the last few months.

Sitting on the edge of her bed, Elizabeth rehearsed the eulogy in her mind, each word a tribute to Father James's impact. She pondered the stories she had chosen to share, each selected to echo his compassion, wisdom, and faith. The responsibility of capturing his essence in words weighed heavily on her, and she felt a compelling duty to convey the depth of his character and the breadth of his influence.

Amid these reflections, Elizabeth also grappled with her own grief. The loss of Father James was a fresh wound, and speaking about him in the past tense was a stark reminder of his absence. Yet, she knew that today was about celebrating his life and carrying his legacy forward. She focused on the comfort she might provide to others mourning his loss and the opportunity to publicly express her gratitude for his guidance and friendship.

She made the familiar walk from the Naval Academy up Newman Street, past Father James's house, and to Saint Mary's Church under a brilliantly blue, cloudless sky. As she entered the church, the soaring arches drew her eyes to the ceiling adorned with intricate wooden beams and softly lit chandeliers. The blue ceiling looked like a beautiful nightscape filled with brightly shining stars. There were dozens of rows of polished wood pews, their surfaces worn smooth by generations of parishioners. The marble altar at the front of the church was a beautiful focal point, adorned with fresh flowers and flanked by tall, white candles that flickered gently.

Elizabeth saw a long line of people gathered to pass by the casket and pay their respects to Father James, who didn't want a full viewing. There were poster boards filled with photographs and the letters Rosemary printed standing on easels lining the interior perimeter of the church. There were photos of Father James as a baby, a kid holding a football with a Gators helmet on his head, shots from his trip to Rome shortly after his ordination, and from each of his stops as a priest. The photos Sister Katherine enclosed with her recent letter were proudly displayed as well. Seeing a handful of drawings from local kids in the parish brought a smile to Elizabeth's face as she sat alone in a pew, gathering her thoughts.

A few minutes later, Father Vincent began walking down the center aisle as the choir sang to begin the Mass.

Here I am, Lord. Is it I, Lord? I have heard you calling in the night. I will go, Lord, if you lead me. I will hold your people in my heart.

After a few moments of silence, Father Vincent asked Elizabeth to come forward to eulogize their mutual friend.

"Good morning," Elizabeth said from the lectern just days after losing Father James.

The morning light poured in from the southeast-facing stained-glass windows of the large, Gothic-style church. The pews were full, dozens of people stood along the sides and in the back, and hundreds more from New Jersey and Arizona tuned in to the livestream. A full choir stood ready from their perch in the balcony by the ornate organ.

"I knew Father James Adams for less than five months," she started. "But to know him for just a few months is to have loved him."

She glanced down at the pews in the front of the church. Walter sat with a handkerchief grasped tightly in his right hand. Rosemary, a rock for anyone who knew her, sat next to him, holding his left hand. She saw the entire prayer group from the Academy sitting together about halfway down on the left side of the center aisle.

"Today, we are not only gathered together in mourning," Elizabeth said. "We are here to celebrate the life of a man who made an impact on each of us and many more who are not able to be with us today. Today, we celebrate a man who was filled with faith—a faith he put into action to help those in need. A man who served his parishioners, a youth group, the Midshipmen, and the Navajo Nation. Father James was more than a priest; he was a mentor, a confidant, and a friend."

Elizabeth paused for a moment to collect herself. She wasn't afraid to show her emotions, but she was determined to make sure they didn't distract from her tribute to Father James. Standing in her full dress uniform with grace and confidence, she commanded the complete attention of the overflowing church. Just before continuing, she noticed Jason Taylor standing alone along the back wall.

"Father James carried with him the scars of his past, the loss of loved ones, and the weight of unresolved pain," she continued. "Yet, he used his own suffering to offer empathy and understanding to everyone he met. His journey was fraught with trials, but like a true shepherd, he used his own struggles to guide and comfort his flock. Eventually, even in his final days, the pain he'd felt and held onto washed away, and when he went home to Christ, he was at peace. In his final hours, he continued to inspire and uplift me as his actions showed the incredible power of reconciliation and love."

She made a point to look once more at Walter and Jason to acknowledge the gift they each gave him. Their presence and request for forgiveness lifted the final burden off a dying man.

"Today, as we bid farewell to this extraordinary man, let us hold tight to the memories, the lessons, and the love he shared with us. Father James taught us to face life's storms with courage, to heal our wounds with love, and to serve others with a joyful heart. He showed us that even in the face of death, there can be peace, forgiveness, and love.

In honoring our friend, Father James, let us commit to carrying forward his legacy. Let us be kinder, love more deeply, and serve with a fervor that mirrored his own. Let us spread the light he kindled in each of us to brighten the world in these times of darkness."

Elizabeth paused. She collected herself before addressing her eyes directly on Father James's casket at the foot of the altar to directly address the departed.

"Father James, thank you for your wisdom, kindness, and unwavering faith," she said to him. "May you rest in peace, knowing that your legacy lives on in the hearts of all those you touched. We are forever grateful for your presence in our lives, and we will always carry your memories with us.

As Elizabeth walked down from the altar, she paused next to the casket and made the sign of the cross. She hoped she had done her friend justice.

The funeral Mass, celebrated by Father Vincent, continued with readings from parishioners and the Gospel from the Book of John. In lieu of a typical homily, Father Vincent gave his own tribute to his late friend and colleague by telling the story of British architect Christopher Wren.

"Upon his death, despite being a famous and world-renowned architect, he was placed in a modest tomb," Father Vincent explained. "He didn't need a grand memorial site or monument. His son had the following inscription put on his tombstone—Lector, si monumentum requiris, circumspice. This translates to 'reader, if you seek a monument, look around.' His monument, his legacy was seen in buildings across London. Right now, in this Church, look around. Look to your left and right. Look behind you."

[239]

He pointed around the church to ensure those gathered followed his direction. He paused as everyone glanced in each direction, a slight murmur filling the church.

"You're looking at Father James's monument," he said. "You are his monument. You are his legacy. Be good to each other. Have faith in God, and put your faith into action with good works. That is the best way to live his legacy every day of your life. It will be a far greater honor to my friend than any grand monument or tombstone."

At the end of Mass, the pallbearers brought Father James from the altar where he'd celebrated Masses, weddings, baptisms, and funerals more times than he could count, down the center aisle one final time. As the congregation followed him outside, the choir in the balcony sang.

And He will raise you up on eagle's wings. Bear you on the breath of dawn. Make you to shine like the sun, and hold you in the palm of His hand.

As Father James's casket was carried past her, Elizabeth felt a profound, almost paralyzing sense of finality wash over her. She watched, her eyes blurred by tears, as the casket moved slowly down the aisle, the weight of her grief grounding her to the spot. Memories of Father James— his gentle guidance, his thoughtful words, and the comfort he had provided to so many—flooded her mind. But, it was the reality of never seeing Father James again, of never hearing his comforting voice or witnessing his compassionate actions, that settled heavily upon her. The weight of this realization made her legs feel weak and her body heavy, as if she might sink right there in the church pew.

Elizabeth didn't cry during the eulogy or when Father Vincent spoke so beautifully about his legacy. But seeing the casket move past her on the way to the back of the church was too much. Rosemary, tears filling her eyes too, turned Elizabeth around and wrapped her in a tight, comforting hug. As the church emptied, Elizabeth stayed glued to her pew, composing herself. Finally, the last to leave, Elizabeth saw Father Vincent motioning for her to join him.

They walked outside and down the church's front steps. Father Vincent took her hand and gave her a reassuring smile.

"Elizabeth," he began, his voice low and earnest, "I want you to know just how much you meant to Father James. He spoke of you often, especially in his final week."

Elizabeth looked up. Despite the words sounding like common post-funeral platitudes, her eyes reflected the appreciation for the words being shared.

"He told me about the night on the bridge," Father Vincent continued.

Elizabeth gulped and felt her heart beating a little faster at the mention of the secret she was prepared to keep.

"He also told me about the difficult situation with Jason's accusation. It was you, Elizabeth, who stood by him through those dark moments. Your strength and your compassion... they were a beacon for him during some very dark days."

Tears that Elizabeth didn't know she had left escaped as she listened, her heart both heavy and comforted by the acknowledgment of the good she'd done for Father James.

Father Vincent gave her hand a reassuring squeeze.

"You saved his life that night, Elizabeth," he said. "And in his final days, when he knew his time here was fading, you brought him comfort and peace that he hadn't felt in a very long time. He was profoundly grateful for your friendship and support."

Elizabeth nodded, struggling to find any words. Father Vincent smiled warmly, his own eyes glistening slightly.

"You did more than you know," Father Vincent told her, looking right into her eyes. "He passed away knowing he was loved, not just by God, but by a true friend. Thank you for being that friend when he needed it most."

Elizabeth abruptly stepped forward and hugged Father Vincent. With the grief of saying goodbye to a friend, she was comforted to know that she had someone who understood what she and Father James had been through. To her, it was a gift from her late friend.

"As you know, we take a vow of poverty as priests," he continued. "So, Father James doesn't have much in terms of a will. But, he asked me to be sure to give this to you after his death."

Without another word, he opened his palm to reveal Father James's rosary. He placed it over Elizabeth's head before giving her another much needed and comforting hug.

Each bead seemed to hold a memory, a moment shared with Father James—a conversation, a smile, a piece of advice. The weight of the rosary around her neck felt heavier than its simple string and beads; it carried the weight of a legacy, a token of trust and friendship.

Elizabeth touched the rosary, feeling the smoothness of each bead under her fingers. It was more than a religious artifact; it was a final gift from someone who had profoundly shaped her path. The realization that Father James had specifically wanted her to have his rosary, an item with profound meaning, deepened her sense of connection to him and the responsibilities he had now entrusted to her.

A swell of gratitude mixed with sorrow filled her heart. She was honored to keep a part of Father James with her yet saddened by the permanence of his departure. This rosary was a symbol of his faith and his struggles. It was a reminder of the spiritual journey they had shared and the unspoken promise to continue the work to which he had dedicated his life. As the cool beads rested against her, Elizabeth felt a renewed commitment to live up to the faith and strength that Father James had seen in her.

There would be no interment today as Father James wished to be buried next to his mother in Florida, honoring a promise he made in her final days. Unsure where to go, Elizabeth started walking toward downtown Annapolis. She walked from the steps of Saint Mary's down Newman Street, passing the house where her friend lived in his final months.

Just before turning left onto Compromise Street, she smiled at the sight and sound of children playing on a playground. She realized that her subconscious was taking her to the Naval Academy Bridge, where she had first met Father James on Christmas.

A few minutes later, she found herself turning from Main Street onto Prince George Street just outside the walls of the Naval Academy. Next to Galway Bay, her favorite restaurant in town, was a small flower shop. She stopped in and bought a small bouquet before heading up College Avenue.

When Elizabeth got to the foot of the bridge, she paused. The bridge brought back complicated memories and strong emotions. It's where she had first met Father James, but it was also where she had to pull a stranger away from the edge in the freezing cold overnight hours of Christmas. She slowly walked to the spot where they met. Cars whizzed behind her in both directions, and she watched people enjoying boat rides on the water below.

She kneeled down and placed the flowers against the railing in front of her. She bowed her head, made the sign of the cross, and said a prayer in the silence of her heart. At that moment, the bridge became more than just a structure of steel and concrete; it was a monument to her journey with Father James, a journey that had started right there with a desperate rescue and blossomed into a genuine friendship. The cold metal of the railing, once a barrier between life and death, now felt like a bridge to something greater, a connection to the memories of a man who had changed her life.

***

Elizabeth crossed the finish line first, to the surprise of absolutely nobody. There was no one in town who stood a chance of beating a Midshipmen cross country star in a local 5K race. She smiled as her friends and family cheered for her and those still finishing the race. The first annual "Caleb Fitzgerald Memorial 5K" was a success. Neighbors and small businesses supported Elizabeth's new initiative by raising $7,100 for her new passion—providing mental health and suicide prevention resources to underserved communities. Runners all wore purple and teal to support the cause, which ended with a barbeque on the Fitzgerald family's dairy farm next to the finish line.

As the event wound down and the last of the day's light faded, Elizabeth stood alone for a moment, looking out over the field where laughter had filled the crisp evening air.

Her heart, which knew the pain of loss all too well, was full. This event, just the beginning of her commitment to giving back, was more than a tribute to her brother; it was an expression of her determination to turn her grief into a positive force.

She felt a strong surge of pride as she considered the overwhelming support she'd received from the community,

[245]

each runner representing a stride towards increased mental health awareness and suicide prevention.

Elizabeth's thoughts drifted to Father James. His influence was palpable in her resolve to aid those battling their darkest moments.

Two weeks later, Elizabeth found herself walking through the terminal at Burlington International Airport on her way to put the money raised at the 5K to use. She flew to Atlanta on her way to Albuquerque, where a volunteer from the Navajo Nation would pick her up and take her to the reservation her late friend had impacted years earlier. After a long day of travel, she made it to the entrance of Saint Michael Indian School by evening.

As Elizabeth stepped out of the car, she was stunned by the canvas of colors in the sky she'd never seen before. The Arizona sunset stretched across the horizon in a spectacular display of deep reds, vibrant oranges, and soft pinks. The vastness of the sky and the boldness of the colors were unlike anything she had ever witnessed on the East Coast.

As Elizabeth stood soaking in the sunset, Sister Katherine approached with a warm smile. Sister Katherine, now in her seventies, carried the gentle marks of age with a dignified grace. Her long hair, mostly silver with traces of its former dark shade, was pulled back into a ponytail.

"I'm so excited to welcome you to the Navajo Nation, Elizabeth," Sister Katherine said, extending her arms to give the young Midshipman a tight hug. "It's so good to meet you."

"Thank you, Sister Katherine," Elizabeth replied, shaking her hand. "Father James told me about how incredible it was here, but this is even more beautiful than I imagined. The sunset—it's just breathtaking."

"It's just one of God's many gifts we enjoy almost every day here on the reservation," Sister Katherine said, her eyes reflecting the hues of the setting sun. "I believe it brings a certain peace, doesn't it? Father James always said the same."

Elizabeth nodded, her thoughts drifting momentarily to her late friend.

"He spoke so fondly of his time here," she told Sister Katherine. "It feels surreal to finally be here, to see what he loved about this place."

"We are deeply grateful for the funds you've raised and your eagerness to help," Sister Katherine continued, leading her toward the school buildings.

"I'm just hoping to make a difference, Sister," Elizabeth said, sincerity lacing her voice. "Father James's work here inspired so many, including me. I'm excited to get started in a place that meant so much to him."

After a quick tour of the school where Father James had worked with Notah, Elizabeth followed Sister Katherine to the convent where she would stay during her visit to the reservation. After a long day of travel and a quick meal,

Elizabeth went to bed exhausted yet excited for her work in the next few days.

The next morning, Elizabeth and Sister Katherine walked to the school and talked about the best ways to help. Sister Katherine was expecting the money raised would help the school buy some much-needed supplies for the guidance counselor's office, but to Sister Katherine's shock, Elizabeth handed her a check for $41,033.

After hearing about the charity run in Vermont, the Saint Mary's community rallied to support Elizabeth's work that honored their late priest. Businesses donated, kids held bake sales, and extra collections were taken at Mass over the next few weeks. The media in nearby Baltimore and Washington D.C. ran stories about Elizabeth's work, and waves of donations poured in. Elizabeth and Sister Katherine were both taken aback by the generosity of strangers.

Sister Katherine was elated that she could now hire another part-time counselor to increase the school's ability to support its students with a particular focus on their mental health needs. Elizabeth promised to find ways each year to send more money to support the school. With joy and gratitude in her heart, Sister Katherine walked Elizabeth down to the counselor's office. Just outside the door was a framed photo hung on the wall for all those who walked past to see. There was a much younger Father James, beaming with pride and his right arm around Notah Nez, clad in his graduation cap and gown.

"I smile every time I see it," Sister Katherine said. "That young man was going nowhere good until Father James got through to him. That's the power of having these resources available to our kids. With your help, more kids on Notah's path will be helped."

Overcome with emotion, she hugged Elizabeth, showing how passionate she was when it came to doing everything in her power to help the children on the reservation.

Over the next few days, Elizabeth helped out during summer school, just as Father James had during his first few days on the reservation. She read to kids, talked to them about what it was like to attend the Naval Academy, and spread the message her friend always preached—finding ways to help others.

Late in the afternoon of her last day on the reservation, Elizabeth found a quiet spot on the edge of the playground where she could watch the children play and listen to their laughter. Her heart was full, not just from the work she had done, but from the connections she had made. She felt a deep sense of fulfillment and a burgeoning responsibility. The generous donation she had facilitated would be put to good use, with plans for the new counselor and expanded mental health resources already taking shape. She imagined the lives that might be turned around, the crises averted, and the futures brightened because of these efforts. It was a legacy that would truly honor Father James's memory—a tangible continuation of his life's work.

Reflecting on the week, she felt an incredible sense of gratitude and purpose. She had come to the Navajo Nation to give, but she left with much more—affirmation for her new passion, a renewed sense of hope, and a promise to herself and to Father James to continue this vital work. As she walked back to the convent, Elizabeth felt a reassuring peace settle over her, confident in the path laid out before her and eager for the journey ahead.

***

After an eventful summer, Elizabeth, now fully recovered from the injury that kept her out of last year's cross country season, was eager to compete again.

As the early September morning air nipped gently at her skin, Elizabeth stood poised among her fellow runners, the breath of each competitor visible in the crisp dawn. Her blue cross country uniform featured a yellow "N" and a matching star on the front. Elizabeth looked around and stood on one leg and held up the other leg behind her back to stretch. She stood close to the starting line, which buzzed with anticipation, surrounded by other runners from Cornell, Georgetown, Saint Joseph's, and her teammates from the Naval Academy, all preparing for the race.

Because of the injury she sustained during her plebe year, the last time she'd raced competitively was during her senior year in high school. She slowed her breathing to ward off the nerves that filled her body. Her thoughts began to drift from the pending race. As she continued stretching, she reflected on her brother, Father James, and her time on the reservation. The anxiety and nerves seemed to fade into the distance. She knew the outcome of one cross country meet wouldn't be what defined her; rather, it would be her service to her country, keeping Father James's legacy alive, and supporting her family that would be the monument she would leave behind at the end of her life.

Elizabeth smiled for a moment, her priorities reorganized in her mind, and refocused her eyes and body on the task immediately before her. With a few moments to spare, she re-tied her favorite neon pink and green sneakers and moved the rosary she wore around her neck under her uniform. She looked to the sky, Caleb and Father James on her mind, and took a cleansing deep breath before getting into position.

As the sound of the starter's pistol cut through the cool air, echoing off the trees and fading into the distance, Elizabeth lunged forward to begin her next journey.

ACKNOWLEDGMENTS

This project would not have been possible without the love, support, and guidance from my family.

I am extremely blessed to have two remarkable parents who continue to guide and inspire me. Mom, you were my first editor and writing teacher. Regardless of the size of the challenge, you taught me to work hard and never stop until I had given it my best. Dad, I am forever thankful for the way you taught me to never give up and follow my dreams. You are both role models for me as a parent, and Abby and Danny are blessed to have you as grandparents.

Growing up, I always tried to keep up with my older brother, Ryan. It wasn't easy because of how successful he was and still is. Ryan, you set a good example for me as a kid, and I still look up to you today.

I live in a family full of teachers. It's given me insight into the difficulties of the job and a genuine love and appreciation for everything teachers give to their students every day. I know I wouldn't be where I am today without the love and guidance I received from teachers throughout my life. Thank you, Sister Pat, for the positive and loving school environment you gave me for nine years and continue to give to my kids today. So many of the teachers you brought into the school had a positive, lasting impact on me, but I especially want to thank Mrs. Marie Kubiak and Ms. Kate Ambrose for sharing their gift of teaching with me.

Thank you to the teachers at Saint Joseph's Prep who built upon the great foundation I was given at SJA. To Dr. Barbara Giuliano and Mr. Bill Conners, thank you for the extra time you put into guiding me during my four years at The Prep. More than 20 years after graduating, The Prep is still helping me. Thanks to Mr. Joseph Coyle, a legendary English teacher, for editing this book.

Thank you, John Lindner, for taking a chance on me and helping me grow as a writer.

I am eternally grateful to my wife, Megan, for her love and support. You are a wonderful teacher, a remarkable mother, and an incredible wife. Thank you for being the first reader of my manuscript and giving me your guidance throughout this project. Without you, this wouldn't have been possible. Abigail and Daniel— your love is the greatest gift I've ever received. Being your Daddy is the best job in the entire world, and I am incredibly proud of the young lady and young man you've become. I love you, today and always!